Service Integration and Management (SIAM®) Fou

Other publications by Van Haren Publishing

Van Haren Publishing (VHP) specializes in titles on Best Practices, methods and standards within four domains:
- IT and IT Management
- Architecture (Enterprise and IT)
- Business Management and
- Project Management

Van Haren Publishing offers a wide collection of whitepapers, templates, free e-books, trainer materials etc. in the **Van Haren Publishing Knowledge Base**: www.vanharen.net for more details.

Van Haren Publishing is also publishing on behalf of leading organizations and companies: ASLBiSL Foundation, BRMI, CA, Centre Henri Tudor, Gaming Works, IACCM, IAOP, Innovation Value Institute, IPMA-NL, ITSqc, NAF, KNVI, PMI-NL, PON, The Open Group, The SOX Institute.

Topics are (per domain):

IT and IT Management
ABC of ICT
ASL®
CATS CM®
CMMI®
COBIT®
e-CF
ISO 20000
ISO 27001/27002
ISPL
IT4IT®
IT-CMF™
IT Service CMM
ITIL®
MOF
MSF
SABSA
SAF
SIAM

Enterprise Architecture
ArchiMate®
GEA®
Novius Architectuur Methode
TOGAF®

Business Management
BABOK® Guide
BiSL® and BiSL® Next
BRMBOK™
BTF
EFQM
eSCM
IACCM
ISA-95
ISO 9000/9001
OPBOK
SixSigma
SOX
SqEME®

Project Management
A4-Projectmanagement
DSDM/Atern
ICB / NCB
ISO 21500
MINCE®
M_o_R®
MSP®
P3O®
PMBOK® Guide
PRINCE2®

For the latest information on VHP publications, visit our website: www.vanharen.net.

Service Integration and Management (SIAM®) Foundation Body of Knowledge

Claire Agutter a.o.

Colophon

Title:	Service Integration and Management Foundation Body of Knowledge (SIAM® Foundation BoK)
Lead author:	Claire Agutter
Contributing authors:	David Baughan (ITSM Value); Nicola Boland-Hill (Sopra Steria); Trisha Booth (Atos); Damian Bowen (ITSM Value); Chris Bullivant (Atos); Harry Burnett (Atos); Alison Cartlidge (Sopra Steria); Simon Dorst (Kinetic IT); Rajiv Dua; Simon Durbin (ISG); James Finister (TCS); Kevin Holland; Dean Hughes (ISG); Andrea Kis(ISG); Anna Leyland (Sopra Steria); Michelle Major-Goldsmith (Kinetic IT); Steve Morgan (Syniad IT); Susan North (Sopra Steria); Charlotte Parnham (Atos); Caroline Trill; Duncan Watkins
Publisher:	Van Haren Publishing, Zaltbommel, www.vanharen.net
NUR code:	981 / 123
ISBN Hard copy:	978 94 018 0102 7
ISBN eBook (pdf):	978 94 018 0103 4
Edition:	First edition, first impression, March 2017
Copyright:	© Van Haren Publishing, 2017

All rights reserved. No part of this publication may be reproduced in any form by print, photo print, microfilm or any other means without written permission by the publisher.

Although this publication has been composed with much care, neither author, nor editor, nor publisher can accept any liability for damage caused by possible errors and/or incompleteness in this publication.

Trademark notices:

SIAM® is a registered trademark of EXIN.
ITIL® is a registered trademark of AXELOS Limited.
IT4IT® is a registered trademark of The Open Group.
COBIT® is a registered trademark of ISACA.
MOF is a registered trademark of Microsoft.
BiSL® is a registered trademark of ASL BiSL Foundation.
ADKAR® is a registered trademark of Prosci.
ISO/IEC 20000® is a registered trademark of ISO.

Preface

Organizations are finding that the sourcing environment is becoming more and more complex. They have moved away from a model where they had outsourced contracts with a single supplier to a model that has specialist service providers – and many of them. This makes supplier management (both internal and external) a challenge in an environment that has to deliver cross-functional, cross-process and cross-provider integration.

Service integration and management (SIAM) has evolved as a result of these challenges. However, many organizations have struggled to truly understand the SIAM approach and adopt it in order to get maximum value from their suppliers.

I have witnessed many organizations realize that they need to have a revised approach to service delivery with effective provision of governance, management, integration, assurance and coordination, but failing to successfully act upon that realization. Exacerbating the situation has been the lack of a single reference point and comprehensive guidance.

The SIAM Body of Knowledge has drawn on the experiences of many organizations and industry experts to create a basic set of SIAM principles from which all sizes and types of organizations can benefit.

I salute the contributors for undertaking this challenge and the tremendous results they have produced. This publication clarifies what SIAM is and its history. The SIAM roadmap clearly sets out the steps that organizations need to follow to effectively adopt a SIAM model. A significant help to organizations on this journey will be the description of the various SIAM structures, when to use each structure and the advantages and disadvantages of each, contained within the BoK.

The publication goes beyond the 'walls' of SIAM to discuss its integration with other practices such as DevOps, Agile, Lean and many more. As an organizational change management zealot, I was pleased to see that SIAM cultural considerations have also been included.

The many challenges that organizations have faced, or will face, such as dealing with legacy contracts, commercial issues, security, cultural fit and behaviors, control and ownership, have all been directly addressed in the BoK.

I recommend this book to every organization considering or already implementing a SIAM model, and I know many would wish they had it in their possession some time ago.

I also recommend this publication for anyone taking the SIAM® Foundation course and exam. It will be an invaluable reference source.

Karen Ferris, Director of Macanta Consulting

Karen Ferris is an internationally acclaimed service management and organizational change management professional with a reputation for providing both strategic and practical advice, assistance and insights for organizations in their implementation and maintenance of efficient and effective business and service management.

She is an author and sought after international speaker. In 2014 she was awarded the lifetime achievement award from itSMF Australia for her contribution to the industry. In 2017 she was voted (by the public) as one of the top 25 thought leaders for technical support and service management in a HDI poll.

Contents

About this Document 10
    Authors and Contributors 10
Document Purpose 10
1. **Introduction to Service Integration and Management (SIAM) 11**
    - 1.1. What is SIAM? 11
    - 1.2. The History of SIAM 25
    - 1.3. The Purpose of SIAM 31
    - 1.4. The Scope of SIAM 32
    - 1.5. SIAM and the Business Strategy 35
    - 1.6. Value to the Organization – the SIAM Business Case 47
2. **SIAM Roadmap** 51
    - 2.1. Discovery and Strategy 53
    - 2.2. Plan and Build 60
    - 2.3. Implement 72
    - 2.4. Run and Improve 76
3. **SIAM Structures** 81
    - 3.1. Externally Sourced Service Integrator 81
    - 3.2. Internally Sourced Service Integrator 85
    - 3.3. Hybrid Service Integrator 88
    - 3.4. Lead Supplier as Service Integrator 90
4. **SIAM and Other Practices** 95
    - 4.1. IT Service Management 95
    - 4.2. Lean 105
    - 4.3. COBIT® 108
    - 4.4. DevOps 110
    - 4.5. Agile, Including Agile Service Management 112

5. SIAM Roles and Responsibilities 117

- 5.1. Roles and the SIAM Roadmap 117
- 5.2. How is a Role Different in a SIAM Ecosystem? 119
- 5.3. Role Description: Customer Organization, including Retained Capabilities 122
- 5.4. Role Description: Service Integrator 124
- 5.5. Role Description: Service Provider 125
- 5.6. Governance Roles 126
- 5.7. Operational Roles 134
- 5.8. The Service Desk in a SIAM Ecosystem 138

6. SIAM Practices 141

- 6.1. People Practices: Managing Cross-functional Teams 141
- 6.2. Process Practices: Integrating Processes across Service Providers 149
- 6.3. Measurement Practices: Enable and Report on End to End Services 153
- 6.4. Technology Practices: Creating a Tooling Strategy 158

7. SIAM Cultural Considerations 164

- 7.1. Cultural Change 165
- 7.2. Collaboration and Cooperation 168
- 7.3. Cross-service Provider Organization 176

8. Challenges and Risks 181

- 8.1. Challenge: Building the Business Case 181
- 8.2. Challenge: Level of Control and Ownership 184
- 8.3. Challenge: Legacy Contracts 185
- 8.4. Challenge: Commercial Challenges 187
- 8.5. Challenge: Security 188
- 8.6. Challenge: Cultural Fit 190
- 8.7. Challenge: Behaviours 191
- 8.8. Challenge: Measuring Success 193
- 8.9. Challenge: Trust/Eliminating Micro-management 194

Appendix A: Glossary of Terms	197
Appendix B Process Guide	203
B.1 What is a Process	204
B.2 Processes and the SIAM Ecosystem	206
B.2.1 Process Guides	207
B.3 Common SIAM considerations	208
B.3.1 Complexity	208
B.3.2 Who owns the End to End Process?	208
B.3.3 Toolset Considerations	209
B.3.4 Data and Information Considerations	209
B.4 Process Guide: Service Portfolio Management	211
B.5 Process Guide: Monitoring and Measuring	213
B.6 Process Guide: Event Management	215
B.7 Process Guide: Incident Management	217
B.8 Process Guide: Problem Management	219
B.9 Process Guide: Change and Release Management	221
B.10 Process Guide: Configuration Management	224
B.11 Process Guide: Service Level Management	227
B.12 Process Guide: Supplier Management	230
B.13 Process Guide: Contract Management	233
B.14 Process Guide: Business Relationship Management	235
B.15 Process Guide: Financial Management	237
B.16 Process Guide: Information Security Management	239
B.17 Process Guide: Continual Service Improvement	242
B.18 Process Guide: Knowledge Management	244
B.19 Process Guide: Toolset and Information Management	246
B.20 Process Guide: Project Management	248
B.21 Process Guide: Audit and Control	250

About this Document

Authors and Contributors

Scopism would like to thank the following people and organizations for their contributions to this document:

Atos

- Trisha Booth
- Chris Bullivant
- Harry Burnett
- Charlotte Parnham

Independents

- Rajiv Dua
- Kevin Holland
- Duncan Watkins
- Caroline Trill

ISG

- Simon Durbin
- Dean Hughes
- Andrea Kis

ITSM Value

- David Baughan
- Damian Bowen

Kinetic IT

- Simon Dorst
- Michelle Major-Goldsmith

Scopism

- Claire Agutter

Sopra Steria

- Nicola Boland-Hill
- Alison Cartlidge
- Anna Leyland
- Susan North

Syniad IT

- Steve Morgan

TCS

- James Finister

Document Purpose

This document introduces service integration and management (SIAM). Its contents are the source material for the EXIN BCS Service Integration and Management Foundation (SIAM®F) certification.

1. Introduction to Service Integration and Management (SIAM)

1.1. What is SIAM?

Service integration and management (SIAM) is a management methodology that can be applied in an environment that includes services sourced from a number of service providers.

SIAM has a different level of focus to traditional multi-sourced ecosystems with one customer and multiple suppliers. It provides governance, management, integration, assurance, and coordination to ensure that the customer organization gets maximum value from its service providers.

SIAM governance operates at three levels in the ecosystem:
- Strategic
- Tactical
- Operational.

SIAM is an evolution of how to apply a framework for integrated service management across multiple service providers. It has developed as organizations have moved away from outsourced contracts with a single supplier to an environment with multiple service providers. SIAM has evolved from the challenges associated with these more complex operating models.

SIAM supports cross-functional, cross-process, and cross-provider integration. It creates an environment where all parties:
- Know their role, responsibilities and context in the ecosystem
- Are empowered to deliver
- Are held accountable for the outcomes they are required to deliver.

SIAM introduces the concept of a service integrator, which is a single, logical entity held accountable for the end to end delivery of services and the business value that the customer receives.

> **Terminology**
> SIAM is the generally accepted acronym for service integration and management.
>
> Other acronyms that are in use are:
> - MSI (Multi Sourcing Integration)
> - SMI (Service Management Integration)
> - SI (Service Integration)
> - SMAI (Service Management and Integration)
> - SI&M (Service Integration & Management).

SIAM can be applied to different sizes and types of organization, and to different industry sectors. Customers that only require a single service provider are unlikely to get the full value from SIAM.

SIAM can be applied to environments that include external service providers only, internal service providers only, or a combination of internal and external service providers. The effectiveness of SIAM and the value it delivers will increase as the number of service providers and the number of interactions between services increase.

Some organizational cultures are more able to adapt to SIAM than others. Effective SIAM requires control to be balanced with trust, devolution of responsibilities, openness, and collaboration across all parties. A transition to SIAM is likely to require significant changes in attitude, behaviour, and culture in ecosystems that previously relied on command and control structures for effective service delivery.

The SIAM methodology encompasses:
- Practices
- Processes
- Functions
- Roles
- Structural elements.

The customer organization will transition to a SIAM model developed from these elements.

1.1.1. The SIAM Ecosystem

There are three layers in a SIAM ecosystem:
1. Customer organization (including retained capabilities)
2. Service integrator
3. Service provider(s).

Each layer has a role as part of effective end to end management of services and the delivery of maximum value. Each layer should have sufficient capability and maturity to fulfil its role.

1.1.1.1. Customer Organization

The customer organization is the end client that is making the transition to SIAM as part of its operating model. It commissions the SIAM ecosystem.

Customer organizations typically contain business units such as human resources, finance, sales, and their own internal IT function. They also have their own customers who use their products and services.

Figure 1 shows the layers of the SIAM ecosystem, and the consumers of services from the customer organization.

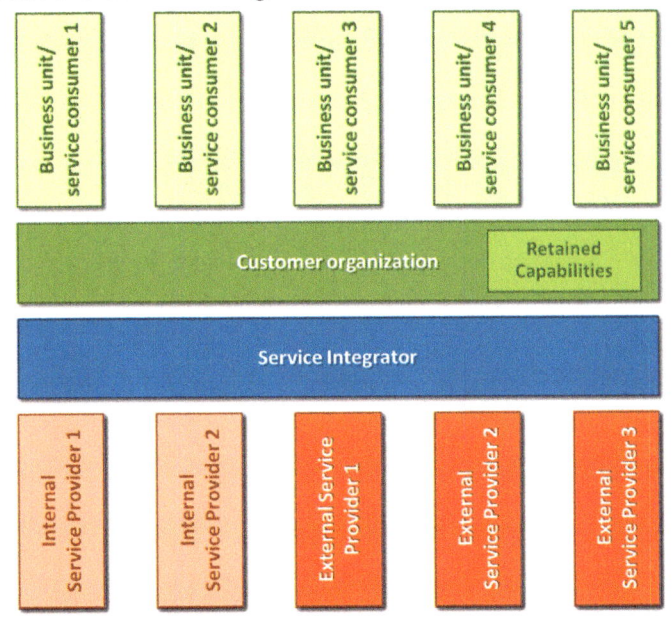

Figure 1 The SIAM layers, including consumers of services from the customer organization

In this document, we use the terms 'customer organization' and 'customer' to mean the commissioning organization.

The customer organization will own the contractual relationships with external service providers, and with any external service integrator.

1.1.1.2. Retained Capabilities

The customer organization will include some retained capabilities. The retained capabilities are the functions that are responsible for strategic, architectural, business engagement and corporate governance activities.

These business-differentiating functions typically remain under the direct control and ownership of the customer organization. Retained capabilities also include any accountabilities and responsibilities that must remain with the customer for legislative or regulatory reasons.

Examples of possible retained capabilities are:
- Enterprise architecture
- Policy and standards management
- Procurement
- Contract management
- Demand management
- Financial and commercial management
- Service portfolio management
- Corporate risk management
- Governance of the service integrator; based on achievement of business outcomes.

The service integrator is independent from the retained capabilities, even if it is internally sourced. Service integration is not a retained capability.

Retained capabilities are sometimes referred to as the 'intelligent client function'.

1.1.1.3. Service Integrator

The service integrator layer of the SIAM ecosystem is where end to end service governance, management, integration, assurance and coordination is performed.

The service integrator layer focuses on implementing an effective cross-service provider organization, making sure that all service providers are contributing to the end to end service. It provides operational governance over the service providers and has a direct relationship with the customer organization and the service providers.

The service integrator layer can be provided by one or more organizations, including the customer organization. If the service integrator layer is provided by more than one organization, it should still be considered as a single logical service integrator.

The service integrator can include one team of people or multiple teams.

1.1.1.4. Service Provider

Within a SIAM ecosystem, there are multiple service providers. Each service provider is responsible for the delivery of one or more services, or service elements, to the customer. It is responsible for managing the products and technology used to deliver its contracted or agreed services, and operating its own processes.

Service providers within a SIAM ecosystem are sometimes referred to as 'towers'. This term implies isolation and a monolithic approach, so the term 'service provider' is used as standard in this document.

Service providers can be part of the customer organization or external to it.

- An external service provider is an organization that is not part of the customer organization. Its performance is typically managed using service level agreements and a contract with the customer organization

- An internal service provider is a team or department that is part of the customer organization. Its performance is typically managed using internal agreements and targets.

Examples of services provided by service providers in a SIAM model include:
- Desktop services/end user computing
- Data centre
- Hosting
- Security
- Network/LAN/WAN
- Cloud services
- Printing services
- Voice and video (VVI)
- Application development, support and maintenance
- Managed services.

If the customer retains its own internal IT capability, this should be treated as an internal service provider, governed by the service integrator.

Service Provider Categories

It can be helpful to categorize service providers in a SIAM ecosystem, to help define their importance to the customer organization and the approach to governing and assuring their services.

There are three common categories of service provider in a SIAM ecosystem:
- Strategic service provider
- Tactical service provider
- Commodity service provider.

SIAM is applied to all three categories, but the nature of the relationship and the amount of management required will be different.

Figure 2 shows a high-level view of the SIAM layers.

Service Integration and Management Foundation Body of Knowledge

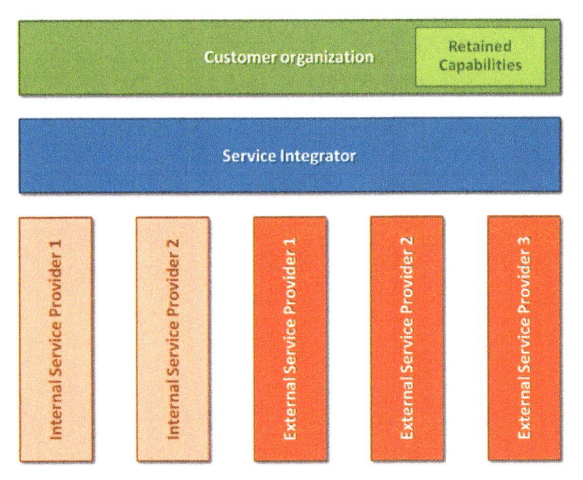

Figure 2 The SIAM layers

The focus, activities and responsibilities of each layer are different. Figure 3 provides an illustration of this.

Strategy
Customer Organization
For example business relationship management, service portfolio, program management, enterprise architecture

Integration
Service Integrator
For example supplier management and coordination, end to end reporting and continual improvement

Delivery
Service Providers
For example application development and support, network services, hosting etc.

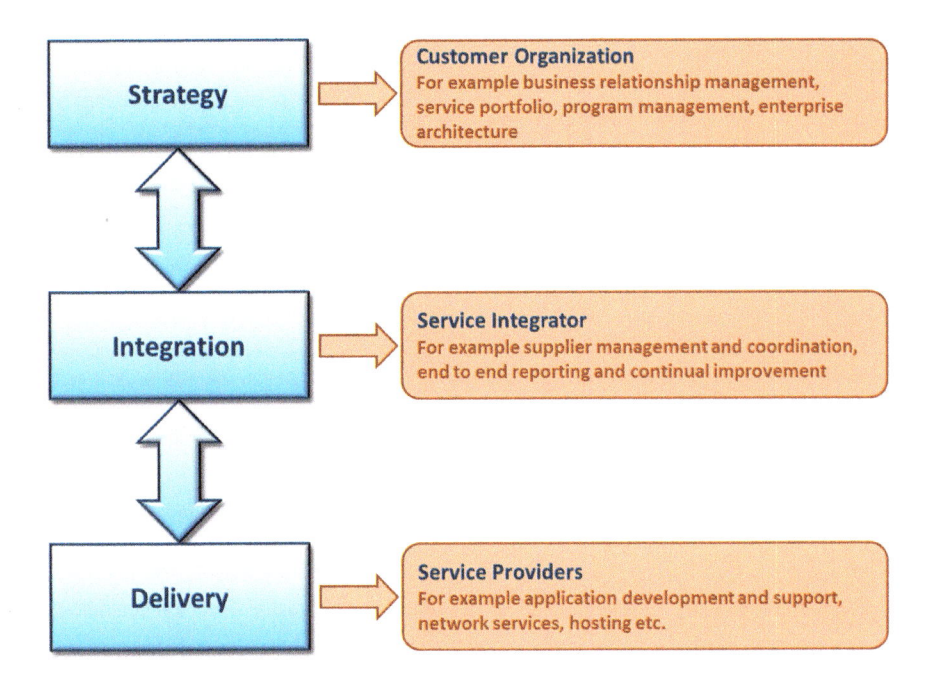

Figure 3 Focus of the SIAM layers

1.1.2. SIAM Practices

Practice: *the actual application or use of an idea, belief, or method, as opposed to theories relating to it.*[1]

SIAM includes specific practices that differentiate it from other management frameworks. These practices support governance, management, integration, assurance, and coordination across the layers.

Examples of practices are described in Section 6: SIAM Practices.
- People practices: managing cross-functional teams
- Process practices: integrating processes across service providers
- Measurement practices: reporting on end to end services
- Technology practices: creating a tooling strategy.

SIAM also draws on other areas of IT and management 'best practice' – see Section 4: SIAM and Other Practices.

1.1.3. SIAM and Processes

Process: *"a documented, repeatable approach to carrying out a series of tasks or activities"*

SIAM itself is not a process; it draws on and uses other management processes.

Most management approaches expect processes to be executed within one organization. In SIAM, these processes may also be executed:
- Across organizations in the same SIAM layer
- Across organizations in different SIAM layers.

Many of the processes used within a SIAM ecosystem are familiar processes like change management and business relationship management. Within a SIAM model, however, these processes require adaptation and augmentation to support integration and coordination

---
[1] Source: Oxford English Dictionary © 2017 Oxford University Press

between the different parties. They also require alignment with the SIAM practices.

Although this is not an exhaustive list, processes used within a SIAM ecosystem can include:
- Audit and control
- Business relationship management
- Change management
- Release management
- Commercial/contract management
- Continual improvement
- Event management
- Financial management
- Incident management
- Request fulfilment
- Service catalogue management
- Information security management
- Knowledge management
- Monitoring, measuring, and reporting
- Problem management
- Project management
- Software asset and configuration management
- Service level management
- Service portfolio management
- Supplier management
- Toolset and information management
- Capacity and availability management
- Service continuity management
- Service introduction, retirement, and replacement.

These processes need to be allocated to the appropriate layers in the SIAM model. This allocation may be different for each implementation of SIAM.

Some processes will span multiple layers. For example: the customer organization and the service integrator can both carry out elements of supplier management; the service integrator and service providers will each have responsibilities in the end to end change management process.

1.1.4. SIAM Functions

Function: *an organizational entity, typically characterized by a special area of knowledge or experience.*[2]

Each organization in the SIAM ecosystem will determine its own organizational structure. This structure will include functions that execute specific processes and practices.

The service integration layer in the SIAM ecosystem has specific functions. These are where the service integrator carries out the activities for governance, management, assurance, integration and coordination.

Whilst these functions may seem similar at a high-level to those from other management methodologies, the activities can be different as they primarily focus on coordination and integration as opposed to operational activities.

The precise functions will vary for different implementations of SIAM, as they are dependent on the definition of roles and responsibilities across the ecosystem, and the detail of the SIAM model that has been adopted.

1.1.5. SIAM Roles

Roles and responsibilities need to be defined, established, monitored and improved within a SIAM ecosystem.

This includes the roles and responsibilities of each:
- Layer
- Organization
- Function
- Structural element.

---

[2] Source: IT Process Wiki

High-level policies for roles and responsibilities are defined during the Discovery and Strategy stage of the SIAM roadmap. More detail is added during the Plan and Build stage.

Roles and responsibilities are allocated to relevant parties during the Implement stage. They are then monitored during Run and Improve and amended as required.

1.1.6. SIAM Structural Elements

Within SIAM, 'structural elements' are organizational entities that have specific responsibilities and work across multiple organizations and layers in the SIAM ecosystem.

These structural elements link the functions with the practices, processes, and roles of SIAM.

The role of the structural elements includes:
- Governance
- Developing and maintaining policies
- Developing and maintaining data and information standards
- Reviewing and improving end to end service performance
- Reviewing and improving capability and maturity
- Identifying, encouraging, and driving continual service improvements and innovation
- Resolving shared issues and conflicts
- Delivering specific projects
- Integration, aggregation and consolidation of data to form an end to end view
- Recognizing and rewarding success.

Structural elements include representatives from the service integrator, the service providers, and, where required, the customer.

Using structural elements helps to establish relationships between the different parties. This encourages communication and collaboration, as attendees work together to achieve shared goals.

The use of structural elements differentiates SIAM from other methodologies, and helps to facilitate the desired outcomes from SIAM.

There are three types of structural element:
1. Boards
2. Process forums
3. Working groups.

1.1.6.1. Boards

Boards perform governance in the SIAM ecosystem.

They are formal decision making bodies, and are accountable for the decisions that they take. Boards will convene regularly, for as long as the SIAM model is in place.

In SIAM, governance activities are carried out by boards operating at strategic, tactical and operational levels. Examples are:
- Strategic: approval of funding, contractual and commercial agreements, and strategy
- Tactical: approval of policies
- Operational: approval of changes to services and processes.

1.1.6.2. Process Forums

Process forums are aligned to specific processes or practices. Their members work together on proactive development, innovations, and improvements.

Forums will convene regularly, for as long as the SIAM model is in place. Their responsibilities include:
- Developing and sharing common working practices
- Developing data and information standards
- Continual improvement
- Innovation.

For example: a problem management process forum can be established with problem management peers from each service provider and the service integrator. They can jointly develop a set of key performance indicators for the problem management process.

Figure 4 shows an example of peer to peer process forums.

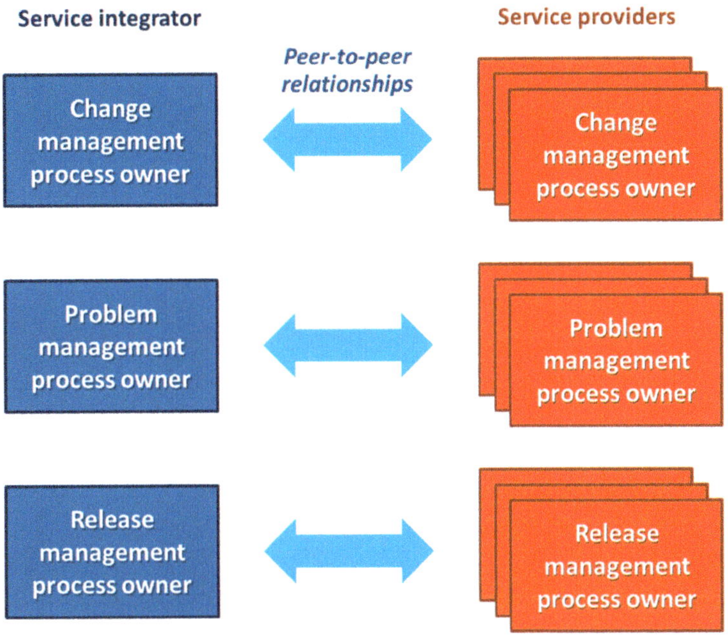

Figure 4 Peer to peer process forums

1.1.6.3. Working Groups

Working groups are convened to address specific issues or projects. They are typically formed on a reactive ad-hoc or fixed-term basis. They can include staff from different organizations and different specialist areas.

For example: an ad-hoc working group could be established with members from several service providers to investigate an intermittent issue with the performance of an integrated service. This could include specialists from capacity management, IT operations, development, problem management and availability management.

Or, a fixed term working group could be established to manage the delivery of an integrated release. The members would be from all layers and from multiple processes and functions.

Process forums and working groups often involve the same people, so can be combined into the same meeting if appropriate. In these combined meetings, it is important to ensure that there is a focus on proactive as well as reactive activities.

1.1.7. SIAM Models

Each organization will develop its own SIAM model, based on the layers in the SIAM ecosystem. The SIAM model that an organization adopts will be influenced by several factors:
- The services that are in scope
- The required outcomes
- The use of proprietary models by externally sourced service integrators.

Because of this, there is no single 'perfect' SIAM model. No model is 'better' than any other, although some may be more suitable to particular implementations than others.

Different organizations adapt models to meet their own needs. All models share common characteristics that are aligned to the methodology described in this BoK.

Figure 5 shows a high-level SIAM model, including the relationships between SIAM layers practices, processes, functions, and structural elements.

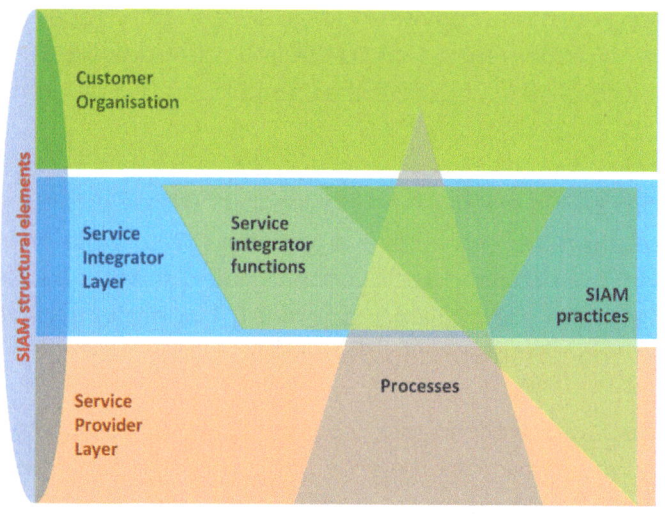

Figure 5. A high-level SIAM model

1.1.8. SIAM Contractual and Sourcing Considerations

Within the SIAM model, the customer owns the contractual relationship with external service providers and any external service integrator.

The service integrator is empowered to act on behalf of the customer, exercising the parts of the contract related to the delivery of the services by the service providers.

The contracts between the service providers and the customer organization must make it clear that the service integrator is the agent of the customer, whether that service integrator is internally sourced or externally sourced.

In many existing customer and provider relationships, standard contracts have limited the ability to transition to SIAM. For SIAM to be effective, the customer organization needs to select the right service providers and have suitable contracts in place.

SIAM contracts are typically shorter and more flexible than traditional IT outsourcing contracts. Targets within the contracts should encourage service providers to work together.

Contracts must also allow flexibility to accommodate future change. They must allow for services and ways of working to adapt to changing business and technology strategies.

Contracts should also encourage all parties to contribute to service improvement and innovation and include targets to support collaboration and innovative behaviour.

1.2. The History of SIAM

1.2.1. SIAM as a Concept

Organizations have been using services delivered by multiple service providers for many years. They have recognized the need for service integration across service providers, and used different approaches to try and achieve end to end service management.

Historically, models for managing this type of ecosystem were proprietary to very large service providers, developed to meet specific client requirements, and rarely shared outside those providers.

In most cases, these service providers also delivered significant systems integration capabilities, but with no clear separation from service integration. These organizations were typically referred to as Systems Integrators (SI) or IT Outsource (ITO) providers.

1.2.2. The Emergence of the Term 'SIAM'

The term 'service integration and management' or SIAM, and the concept of SIAM as a management methodology originated in around 2005 from within the UK public sector, which was also the source of other best practice methodologies such as ITIL®.

The methodology was initially designed for the Department of Work and Pensions to obtain better value for money from services delivered by multiple service providers, and specifically to separate service integration capabilities from systems integration and IT service provision.

This new approach reduced the duplication of activities in the service providers, and introduced the concept of a 'service integrator'. This new service integration capability provided governance and coordination to encourage service providers to work together to drive down costs and improve service quality.

SIAM was viewed as a methodology, not a function. Within the methodology, a service integrator provided a set of service integration capabilities.

The SIAM methodology that was emerging facilitated collaboration between the various service providers, and management of interfaces between them. The service integrator was 'one step above' the service provider layer.

Processes were used in the SIAM ecosystem to define activities, inputs, outputs, controls, and measurements. The methodology allowed individual service providers to act autonomously and define the specific mechanisms that enabled those activities. These were then audited and assured by the service integrator.

Figure 6 shows a simple view of the SIAM model.

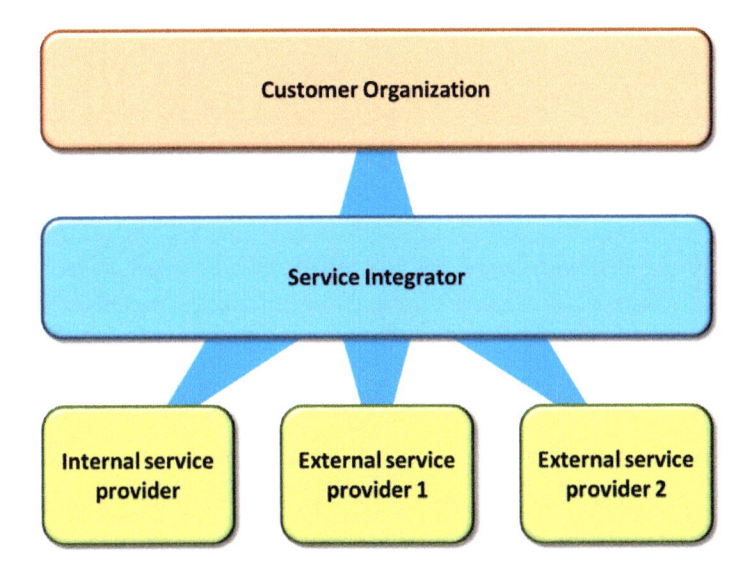

Figure 6. A simple view of a SIAM ecosystem

1.2.3. Growth and Adoption of SIAM within UK Government

In 2010, the UK Government published a new information and communications technology (ICT) strategy. This included moving away from large prime supplier contracts to a more flexible approach using multiple service providers and cloud based solutions.

A paper was published in support of this strategy that set out a new approach for service management governance and organization. The proposal was to appoint an appropriate service management framework to coordinate multiple services, providers and consumers in a secure and seamless lifecycle of service delivery and improvement. This accelerated the development and awareness of SIAM both in the UK public sector and elsewhere. This acceleration led to the publication in 2012 of the UK Government 'Cross Government Strategic SIAM Reference Set'. This was developed from experience and expertise in SIAM from the Department of Work and Pensions, Ministry of Justice, NHS

Connecting for Health, and the Government Procurement Service. Figure 7 shows the SIAM Enterprise Model from this reference set.

The aim of the reference set was to enable transformation in UK public sector organizations to a disaggregated, multi-sourced, multi-service environment.

The reference set described a wide range of SIAM capabilities and a suggested enterprise model, but encouraged adaptation to suit local requirements.

This was the first widely available description of SIAM. Its publication rapidly increased the awareness, development, and discussion of SIAM worldwide.

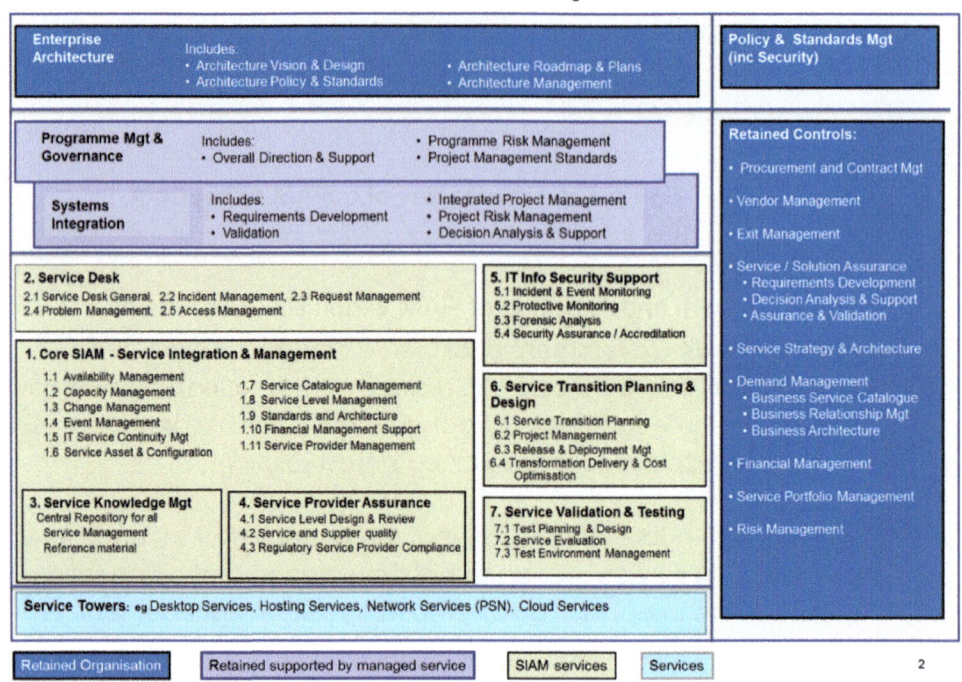

Figure 7 SIAM Enterprise Model from Service Integration & Management (SIAM) Framework Cross Government Reference Set, October 2012

The contemporary UK Government Service Design Manual advised that:

"The level of service integration will differ depending on the complexity of the business services and/or customers that are being supported, and the complexity of the services that are being delivered to those businesses. As the services and businesses become more critical or complex, the level of service integration becomes deeper.

The design of the service integration function will differ by department. It may be completely operated in-house. Or it might consist of a thin in-house capability ultimately responsible for the integrated end to end operation and management of quality IT services, underpinned by outsourced integration services for specific elements – for example performance monitoring, service desk, or service level reporting. Particularly for smaller departments and simple services, care needs to be taken not to over-engineer the service integration approach – effective use of commodity standards-based IT should mean that integration and support requirements are much less onerous than managing a locked-down bespoke system."[3]

1.2.4. Recent History

More recently, the development of approaches to SIAM and its adoption has increased significantly. This has been driven by strategic factors including:

- A worldwide need to improve value
- A desire to remove reliance on single suppliers
- The need for effective controls
- A desire for the ability and flexibility to use 'best of breed' service providers and services, including the use of commodity cloud-based services.

The development and adoption of SIAM has been accompanied by an increase in the number of publications on SIAM, and the number of commercial organizations offering service integration capabilities; many of whom have their own model.

---

[3] Source https://www.gov.uk/service-manual

> "Against a backdrop of increased business and IT complexity, the IT service provider is faced with a challenge to deliver more with less. Customers demand IT cost transparency and demonstrated value. Additionally,
> multi-sourced service delivery is the new reality for many. Both customers and users are demanding innovative technology solutions and access to each providers' specialisms, but do not necessarily want to be presented with the issues that controlling the complex web of multiple providers brings.
>
> The multi-provider delivery models evident in many modern enterprises have created an interest in the benefits SIAM can bring. More and more customers are calling for better defined and more cohesive control structures that will allow the management of multiple service providers in a consistent and efficient way. They demand performance across a portfolio of services that meets the needs of the users and can be flexed as the needs change."
>
> Source: Who is the King of SIAM? Whitepaper, Simon Dorst, Michelle Major-Goldsmith, Steve Robinson
> Copyright © AXELOS 2015. All rights reserved

Whilst SIAM itself may not be new, what is new is the recognition that SIAM is essential to support the delivery of value in multi-supplier ecosystems.

As more and more organizations move to this way of delivering services, the need for a standardized methodology for service integration has become apparent.

1.3. The Purpose of SIAM

> *"Effective SIAM seeks to combine the benefits of best-of-breed based multi-sourcing of services with the simplicity of single sourcing, minimising the risks inherent in multi-sourced approaches and masking the supply chain complexity from the consumers of the services. SIAM is therefore appropriate for businesses that are moving to or already have a multi-sourced environment. The benefits of a well-designed, planned and executed SIAM model can be realized by businesses that use multiple external suppliers, a mix of internal and external suppliers, or several internal suppliers. SIAM is therefore appropriate for most of today's businesses."*
>
> Source: An Example ITIL®-based Model for Effective Service Integration and Management Whitepaper, Kevin Holland
> Copyright © AXELOS 2015. All rights reserved

SIAM can, at first glance, seem to be simply an adaptation of commonly understood service management approaches such as ITIL®, COBIT®, the Open Systems Interconnect (OSI) model or the Microsoft Operations Framework (MOF). Where SIAM differs is that it acknowledges and focuses on the specific challenges associated with multi-sourced service delivery models.

The service integrator provides the customer with a single point of accountability and control for the integrated delivery of services. This is achieved through the definition and application of controls within a robust governance methodology that also provides the necessary coordination between the service providers within the SIAM ecosystem. The service integrator also drives collaboration and improvement across the service providers, acting on behalf of the customer.

The service integrator takes ownership of these activities on behalf of the customer, allowing the customer organization to focus on the activities necessary for their business, rather than focusing on service providers and technology.

The service integrator manages the complexities of dealing with multiple service providers, allowing the customer to benefit from their specialisms and capabilities without incurring any additional management burden.

The application of the SIAM methodology creates an ecosystem where all parties involved in the delivery of the services are clear about their roles and responsibilities and are empowered to deliver within those boundaries.

SIAM also provides an understanding of the necessary interactions between the services and the service providers, and the techniques to effectively manage those interactions. This facilitates the coordination of delivery, integration and interoperability.

The service integrator provides assurance of the performance of individual service providers and over the end to end service, ensuring that the expected outcomes are delivered to the customer.

SIAM enables the flexibility and innovation necessary to support the pace of change demanded by today's fast moving organizations.

1.4. The Scope of SIAM

The scope of SIAM will vary from organization to organization. For the customer organization to derive any benefit from a transition to a SIAM model, the service(s) that are in scope must be defined.

This service definition makes it clear what is being governed, assured, integrated, coordinated and managed by the service integrator.

For each service within the scope of SIAM, these areas need to be defined:
- Service outcomes, value, and objectives
- The service provider(s)
- The service consumer(s)
- The service characteristics, including service levels
- The service boundaries
- Dependencies with other services
- Technical interactions with other services
- Data and information interactions with other services.

A service model should be created that shows the hierarchy of services. This hierarchy must clearly identify:
- Services that are directly consumed by the customer organization
- Underpinning services and dependencies.

Figure 8 shows an example of a service model showing the service hierarchies.

The model shows how business needs in the customer organization are met by service provider services (lettered), and how in turn they are dependent on one or more supporting services (numbered) which may be delivered by an alternative provider.

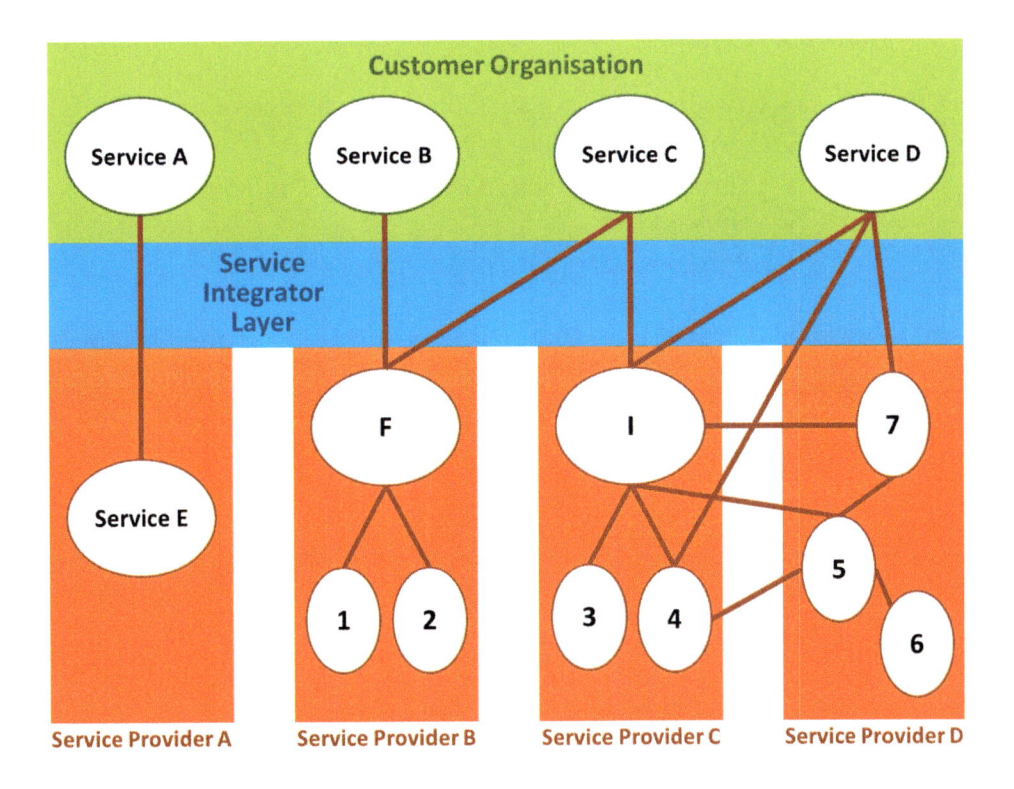

Figure 8. Service model showing hierarchy of services

1.4.1.1.   Types of Service

SIAM can be applied to both IT services and technologies and non-IT services. Historically, it has mainly been adopted for IT services.

SIAM can be applied to managed services and cloud services, as well as to more traditional IT services like hosting or end user computing.

Different organizations will have different types of services within the scope of their SIAM model. Some models may only include services that were previously provided by internal IT, as part of a strategy to outsource these services to external organizations.

Others may include a wide range of externally provided services, and retain their internal IT department as an internal service provider. The customer organization will determine the scope in line with their strategy and requirements.

Examples of IT services include:
- Office productivity applications
- Customer relationship management systems
- Networks
- Bespoke customer applications.

Examples of non-IT services that can be within the scope of SIAM are business processes such as sales order management, payroll processing, and consumer help desks.

Cloud Services

SIAM can be applied to commodity services provided from the cloud. These include:
- Software as a Service (SaaS)
- Platform as a Service (PaaS)
- Infrastructure as a Service (IaaS).

Service providers for cloud services use the same delivery models for all their customers. It is therefore unlikely that they will adapt their ways of working to align with a customer's specific SIAM requirements, or accept governance from the service integrator.

If this is recognized, and the service integrator can adapt to their approach while still delivering customer outcomes, SIAM can still be effective for these services.

1.5. SIAM and the Business Strategy

1.5.1. Why Change?

Without effective service integration, many of the benefits anticipated from services delivered by multiple service providers can remain unrealized.

Transforming an organization to a SIAM model ensures that critical artefacts are developed as part of the SIAM roadmap. These will include:

- A clear design for how the overall end to end service will operate and integrate
- A standard governance approach
- Definition of accountability for the integrated service
- An end to end performance management and reporting framework
- Coordination between service providers
- Integration between the processes of different service providers
- Definition of roles and responsibilities
- Definition of ownership and coordination for incidents and problems that involve multiple suppliers.

Organizations must be clear about why they want to adopt SIAM. Transitioning to a SIAM-based model is not an easy task. It will require investment, and changes for all involved parties. The changes will affect areas including:

- Attitude, behaviour, and culture
- Processes and procedures
- Capabilities
- Organizational structures
- Resources
- Knowledge
- Tools
- Contracts.

Senior level sponsorship and management commitment will be essential. Without management commitment, the transformation to a SIAM model is unlikely to succeed.

There are organizations for whom SIAM is not appropriate. Before any organization embarks on a transition to SIAM, it must fully understand SIAM and the benefits it could derive. This will enable it to make a value-based judgement.

The organization can gain this understanding in one of three ways, or in combination:
- Educate and train the staff who are leading on SIAM discovery and strategy in the SIAM methodology
- Seek help from outside the organization, either from similar organizations or from organizations experienced in SIAM adoption
- Recruit new staff who have the required understanding and experience.

1.5.2. Drivers for SIAM

In this context, a driver is defined as *"something that creates and fuels activity, or gives force and impetus"*[4]

These drivers are the triggers that create an organization's desire to move to a SIAM model. Understanding the drivers for SIAM will help an organization to gain clarity of purpose.

The drivers will be used to create a business case for the transition to SIAM. They will also help the organization to maintain focus throughout the SIAM roadmap.

---

[4] Source: Collins English Dictionary – Complete and Unabridged, 12th Edition 2014 © HarperCollins Publishers 1991, 1994, 1998, 2000, 2003, 2006, 2007, 2009, 2011, 2014

The Challenges of Delivery in a Multi-Service Provider Ecosystem

Service providers play a crucial role in helping a customer deliver its business outcomes. Poorly delivered services directly affect the customer's outcomes, and the service it can offer to its own customers.

This is true whether the services are delivered by one service provider or multiple service providers. However, the challenges of successful delivery are greater when there are multiple service providers, owing to increases in complexity and the interactions that need to take place between service providers.

Consider these scenarios that illustrate how poor service provision can have wider consequences:

- A hospital has booked in a patient to have an extensive medical scan. The medical machinery has stopped working and the cause of failure is unknown. The patient's appointment must be re-scheduled. Will the delay to this appointment have a negative impact on the patient's health?

- A motoring organization cannot despatch a patrolman to assist a lone female motorist and her small child on a busy freeway because their command and control systems are unavailable due to a failed system change. The organization doesn't know which patrolmen are available or where they are. To how much risk is the woman and her child exposed, and for how long?

- An online retailer is unable to cope with the increase in transactions prior to the holiday season. This makes its retail platform slow down, unnecessarily reject payments and at times show as unavailable. Will customers accept this, or buy their goods and services elsewhere?

- A hastily implemented, partially tested update to a travel agent's booking system has caused the personal information of its customers (including credit card details) to be hacked. The press has found out and is publishing worst-case scenarios of identity theft and potential financial impact for the customers. Will the reputation of this travel agent recover enough to remain a viable business?

There are generic drivers for SIAM that can be tailored for each organization. These can be placed into five driver groups:
1. Service satisfaction
2. Service and sourcing landscape
3. Operational efficiencies
4. External drivers
5. Commercial drivers.

1.5.2.1. Service Satisfaction Drivers

These are drivers related to the level of satisfaction the customer has with the services that it receives, and the level of satisfaction that is expected.

There are seven drivers related to service satisfaction:
1. Service performance
2. Service provider interactions
3. Clarity of roles and responsibilities
4. Slow pace of change
5. Demonstration of value
6. Lack of collaboration between service providers
7. Delivery silos.

Service Performance

Customers expect guaranteed service performance and availability, irrespective of who provides the service.

On some occasions, customers in a multi-service provider ecosystem can experience dissatisfaction with the level of service they receive, even though each of the service providers report that they are achieving their individual service level targets.

One example is incident resolution times, where the time taken to pass an incident from one service provider to another is not considered in the service level calculation.

Without effective governance, coordination and collaboration, there will be service performance issues including:
- A lack of transparency for the end to end service
- Incomplete understanding of, and inability to report on, end to end service performance
- No management of service levels across the end to end service
- Service performance that is not aligned to business requirements.

Service Provider Interactions

In a multi-service provider environment, service users might have to interact separately and differently with each internal and external service provider.

For example, one service provider might only accept contact from users by telephone, another only by email, and another only by an internet portal.

Clarity of Roles and Responsibilities

Roles, responsibilities and accountabilities can be unclear in an ecosystem that has multiple service providers. The responsibility and accountability for the delivery of services is often held in several different places.

Some customer departments may have the primary relationship with a service provider; for example, the payroll department with the external provider of payroll services. Some service providers may need to have relationships with multiple customer departments; for example, the hosting provider with IT operations, the engineering department and the application development department.

Without effective governance and coordination, a culture can develop where there is no ownership of issues, leading to customer dissatisfaction and loss of perceived value.

For example, a customer frequently experiences slow performance of a business service. This service underpinned by several technical services from different service providers. Every provider says that its service is performing correctly and another service provider must be responsible.

Slow Pace of Change
Customers expect changes to be made quickly to meet business requirements.

They also expect that new services, new service providers, and new technologies can be introduced rapidly and integrated with existing services to meet demanding timescales.

Demonstration of Value
Customers expect that services will deliver the outcomes they require, at a reasonable level of cost and quality. In many organizations, the IT department is not able to demonstrate this value to the customer.

Lack of Collaboration between Service Providers
As the number of parties involved in service delivery increases, so does the need for collaboration.

The requirement is no longer just about a one-way relationship between a service provider and the customer, but a network of relationships between multiple service providers who all need to work together to provide a customer-focused service.

External service providers have their own commercial interests and drivers, which can conflict with the goals of the customer and other service providers.

An example of this is where a business service received by the customer relies on the integration of several services from different service providers. An individual service provider may only be concerned with the availability of the service elements for which it is responsible.

If a service provider does not consider how its service interacts with other providers' services, it could make changes that stop the integrated service working.

Delivery Silos
Delivery silos can exist where there are multiple internal or external service providers. Each service provider focuses only on its own goals and outcomes.

These silos isolate service providers, processes and departments. Their impact includes:
- Duplication of work
- Lack of knowledge sharing
- Increased cost of service provision
- Potential for degraded service performance
- Inability to identify service improvements.

A blame culture can arise between the service providers due to the lack of co-operation between silos. When a service is faulty, each silo focuses on proving it is not at fault, rather than working with other silos to correct the fault.

1.5.2.2. Service and Sourcing Landscape Drivers
These are drivers related to the nature, number, and types of services and service providers, and the complexity of the interactions between them.

There are five drivers related to the service and sourcing landscape:
1. External sourcing
2. Shadow IT
3. Multi-sourcing
4. Increase in the number of service providers
5. Inflexible contracts.

External Sourcing
Many of the traditional frameworks and practices used to manage IT services were designed for an environment where most of the services were developed and supported internally. However, the way that many customers source their services has fundamentally changed.

Rather than the former insourced approach, many organizations have made the strategic decision to source applications and services externally.

External sourcing of services may enable a customer to reduce costs by realizing the benefits of competition amongst a wider network of service providers. This sourcing approach can also provide the customer with access to best in class capabilities.

These services often include specialized and cloud-based commodity services. The customer expects that all services will be fully integrated with other services that they consume.

Shadow IT
Shadow IT describes IT services and systems commissioned by business departments, without the knowledge of the IT department (sometimes referred to as 'stealth IT').

These services are commissioned to meet a business requirement, but can cause problems when they require connectivity and alignment with the other services consumed by the customer.

Multi-sourcing
Many organizations have made a strategic decision to transition from single-sourcing to multi-sourcing and multiple delivery channels.

This transition often results in a mix of internal and external sourcing. Multi-sourcing can reduce many of the risks and issues associated with being over-reliant on a single service provider. These risks include:
- Slow pace of change and low levels of innovation
- High cost of services when benchmarked against competitors
- Reliance on specific technology platforms
- Inability to take advantage of new service offerings, service providers or technologies that are available elsewhere
- Long term contractual restrictions
- Lack of control over services
- Lack of service knowledge in the customer organization
- High risk to service continuity during a transition to a new service provider
- Cost of the transition to a new single service provider
- A risk that the service provider may go out of business.

Increase in the Number of Service Providers
The number of service providers in the market is increasing. More and more options are available to customer organizations that are evaluating different sourcing approaches.

Inflexible Contracts
Lengthy, inflexible contracts with service providers lock in customers and prevent them accessing technology developments and innovative practices.

Moving to a SIAM model will typically include shorter, more flexible contracts that allow customers to add and remove service providers, and adapt how they work with existing service providers.

1.5.2.3. Operational Efficiencies Drivers

These are drivers that relate to improvements and efficiencies for the end to end delivery of services, and the potential to create operational efficiencies through standardization and consolidation.

There are four drivers related to operational efficiencies:
1. Disparate service management capabilities
2. Data and information flows
3. Data and information standards
4. Tooling.

Disparate Service Management Capabilities
In an environment with multiple service providers, each of them will maintain its own service management capability. The customer will also need to retain service management capabilities, which interact with the service providers.

This can result in:

- Duplication of resources and activities
- Low utilization in some areas and high utilization in others
- Inconsistent levels of capability and maturity
- No sharing of knowledge
- Inconsistent processes and procedures
- A blame culture between teams.

These can result in increased costs and degraded service performance for the customer organization.

Data and Information Flows
In an environment with multiple service providers, data and information will be transferred between parties during end to end service delivery.

If the data and information flows are not mapped and understood, the flow can be interrupted, leading to service performance issues and operational inefficiencies.

The 'integration' element of the SIAM methodology manages the service from end to end. This requires an understanding of all data and information sources and interactions between all parties[5].

Mapping data and information flows provides an insight into the boundaries between the different service providers. This knowledge can then be used to create integrated flows of data and information.

SIAM is then used to manage and coordinate these flows. This enables end to end delivery of the required level of service to the customer.

Data and Information Standards
If data and information standards are not consistent across all service providers, then extra effort will be required when data and information are exchanged between service providers and with the customer.

A common data dictionary, introduced as part of an integrated approach to service management, would include:
- Incident severity, categorization and recording
- Service levels and service reporting
- Requests for change
- Capacity and availability recording
- Management report formats
- Knowledge artefacts.

---

[5] Techniques like OBASHI™ can be used to map data flows to support service integration and management

Tooling
Service providers will have their own toolsets to support their internal processes.

When there is a requirement to exchange data and information with other providers and the customer, lack of integration between toolsets can create problems.

Without a design for interoperability these exchanges can be inefficient, leading to:

- Re-entry of data and information by the receiving party (the 'swivel chair approach')
- A requirement to translate data and information
- Inadvertent alteration of data and information
- Loss of data and information
- Time delays in the exchange between the parties, resulting in a poor service experience.

> **The Swivel Chair Approach**
> The 'swivel chair approach[6]' is a colloquial term for manually entering data into one system and then entering the same data into another system. The term is derived from the practice of the user turning from one system to another using a swivel chair.

1.5.2.4. External Drivers

These are drivers that are imposed from outside the organization. The organization must respond to these drivers in some way.

There are two drivers related to external factors:

1. Corporate governance
2. External policy.

Corporate Governance
Many customers have corporate governance requirements which demand clarity over the responsibilities of service providers and the controls that are applied to them. An example is the Sarbanes Oxley

---

[6] Source: http://www.webopedia.com/TERM/S/swivel_chair_interface.html

Act passed in the United States of America in 2002 to protect investors from fraudulent accounting activities.

Effective corporate governance requires a definition of roles, responsibilities, accountabilities and interactions between all parties and systems at a far more granular level than in the past.

External Policy
For some organizations, the use of SIAM is mandated under a policy created outside the customer organization.

Policy drivers apply to:

- Public sector organizations affected by government or state policies
- Public sector service providers affected by government or state policies
- Private sector organizations that are part of a larger group that has adopted SIAM as part of its strategy.

1.5.2.5. Commercial Drivers

These drivers apply to organizations who want to offer commercial services related to SIAM.

There are two drivers related to commercial factors:
1. Service providers
2. Service integrators.

Service Providers
When a customer organization adopts SIAM, it will need its service providers to align to its SIAM model.

The delivery models of many traditional providers do not align with SIAM models, because they do not consider the requirements for integration with other service providers and a service integrator.

If these service providers want to be able to compete for business in SIAM ecosystems, they must make changes to how they deliver their services.

Changes will affect:
- Tooling
- Processes and procedures
- Process interfaces
- Data dictionaries and standards
- Service reporting
- Governance approaches
- Data and information standards
- Commercial and contractual standards.

Service Integrators
Some organizations want to provide service integration capabilities to customers. They might act as an externally sourced or hybrid service integrator, or they might provide specialist support during one or more stages of the SIAM roadmap:

- Discovery and Strategy
- Plan and Build
- Implement
- Run and Improve.

1.6. Value to the Organization – the SIAM Business Case

Any organization that is considering a transition to SIAM needs to understand the expected benefits. Clarity on these benefits will form the basis for developing the organization's business case for SIAM.

Benefits can be a mixture of tangible (for example: cost savings) and intangible (for example: improved customer service).

The benefits and costs will be different for each organization. They depend on many factors, including:
- Drivers
- Required business outcomes
- Services in scope
- The customer organization's role in the SIAM ecosystem
- Budget

- Organizational culture
- Appetite for risk
- The legacy contracts in place and their flexibility to accommodate new ways of working.

The costs that will be incurred need to include not just cost of service under a SIAM model, but also the cost of the transition project to achieve the change. There will also be costs associated with developing any capabilities or artefacts which the organization does not currently have, but which will be required to operate within a SIAM ecosystem.

An organization should consider its own drivers to achieve the necessary clarity for the anticipated business benefits.

There are generic benefits that are likely to be relevant to most organizations making the transition to SIAM. The benefits can be placed into four groups:
1. Improved service quality
2. Optimized costs and increased value
3. Improved governance and control
4. Improved flexibility and pace.

When defining the expected benefits, organizations should consider how long it will take for them to be delivered. It can be some time after the transition is complete before benefits start to be realized.
A SIAM model leverages experience and input from multiple service providers. It delivers benefits from collaboration between service providers, and from competitive tension between them.

1.6.1. Improved Service Quality
Improving service quality often forms part of a SIAM business case. Benefits related to service quality can include:
- A shift in focus from satisfying contractual targets to focus on innovation and satisfying perceived business need
- Consistent achievement of service levels, including end to end:
    - Incident and problem resolution times
    - Service availability
    - Service reliability

- Improvements in customer satisfaction with the services
- The customer can concentrate on delivering its business outcomes, and have confidence in its supporting services
- Improved quality in the delivery of changes, integrated across service providers
- Improved flow of end to end processes, sometimes referred to as 'SIAM cadence'
- Consistency in how end users interact with service providers
- Consistent and understandable management information about the services
- Access to best of breed services and service providers
- Development and sharing of knowledge and best practice
- Continual service improvement.

1.6.2. Optimized Costs and Improved Value

The business case for SIAM must include the costs associated with the transition to a new way of working. The service integrator layer can add additional cost to an organization, whether it is externally sourced or provisioned using internal resources.

However, the increased value associated with a transition to SIAM, and the potential for cost optimization in the service provider layer, should balance out or exceed any overall cost increases.

If SIAM is correctly designed and implemented, it will provide better service value, with both tangible and intangible benefits.

Benefits in this group include:
- Cost optimization from:
  - Innovation
  - An understanding of the true cost and value of each service and service provider
  - Competitive tension between service providers
  - Best use of skilled (and often scarce resources)
  - Reduced costs of process execution
  - Identification and removal of duplication of resources and activities
- Improved value for money for individual services
- Consistent performance from all service providers, leading to improved efficiency

- Improved management of resources and capacity
- Faster response to changing business needs
- Faster access to new technologies and services
- Contract optimization and the potential for shorter term, more effective contracts
- Flexibility to accommodate change.

1.6.3. Improved Governance and Control

SIAM provides an opportunity to apply consistent governance and control over all service providers, both internal and external. Governance and control benefits include:

- Consistent and visible definition and application of a governance framework
- Consistent assurance of services and service providers
- A single point of ownership, visibility, and control of services
- Clearly defined services, roles, responsibilities, and controls
- Improved management of service provider performance
- The ability to benchmark between service providers
- Contract optimization and standardisation related to governance and control
- Improved visibility, understanding and management of service risks.

1.6.4. Improved Flexibility

If correctly designed and implemented, SIAM can provide the flexibility that is necessary to support changing business requirements, balanced with an appropriate level of control.

The benefits in this group include:

- Effective and timely introduction of new and changed services and service providers
- The flexibility to replace poorly performing or uneconomic service providers
- The ability to rapidly accommodate changes to services, technologies, and business requirements
- Increased ability to manage commodity services in a consistent way
- Increased ability to scale service provision.

2. SIAM Roadmap

This roadmap outlines an example plan for the implementation of SIAM as part of an organization's operating model.

Using a roadmap for the implementation has several benefits, including:
- Defining the SIAM requirements
- Providing a planning framework
- Determining the most appropriate SIAM structure and SIAM model
- Guiding the implementation
- Directing ongoing continual improvement.

There are four stages in the SIAM roadmap:

1. Discovery and Strategy
2. Plan and Build
3. Implement
4. Run and Improve.

For each stage, this section provides examples of:

1. Objectives
2. Triggers
3. Inputs
4. Activities
5. Outputs.

Whilst the activities are presented here in a sequential manner, many are likely to be iterative or may even be undertaken in parallel.

High-level requirements are defined in the first stage. These are then further developed in the second stage, before being implemented in the third stage. The fourth stage is where the SIAM model is operated and continually improved.

In many cases, the roadmap will be executed iteratively, with a checkpoint at the end of each stage. The checkpoint should review areas including:
- The actual outputs from the stage against those intended
- Risks
- Issues
- Plan for the next stage.

This information should be used to validate decisions taken earlier in the roadmap. It might highlight potential issues, requiring a return to an earlier stage for further work.

> **An Example of an Iterative Roadmap**
>
> In the Discovery and Strategy stage, a customer organization might propose an internally sourced service integrator.
>
> In the second stage, it formulates a plan and designs its SIAM model to support this structure.
>
> However, during the third stage it discovers that it is unable to recruit the necessary resources. It returns to the first stage to review its strategy, and changes it to apply the hybrid service integrator structure.
>
> The Plan and Build stages must then be revisited.

Many organizations use outside assistance during the execution of their SIAM roadmap. This can be helpful during the transition to SIAM, but the customer organization needs to ensure that the model being used by the external organization is suitable for its needs.

If outside help is required, it is a good idea to have a commercial boundary between an organization that is assisting with the Discovery and Strategy and Plan and Build stages, and any external service integrator.

2.1. Discovery and Strategy

2.1.1. Objectives

The Discovery and Strategy stage initiates the SIAM transformation project, formulates key strategies, and maps the current situation. This enables the customer organization to:

- Determine what it intends to source internally
- Consider any additional skills and resources that may be required
- Determine what it would like to source externally
- Understand the expected benefits.

The objectives for this stage are to:

1. Establish the SIAM transition project
2. Establish a governance framework
3. Define the strategy and outline model for SIAM and the services in scope
4. Analyze the current state of the organization, including skills, services, service providers, tools and processes
5. Analyze the marketplace for potential service providers and service integrators.

2.1.2. Triggers

There are many reasons for organizations to consider adopting a SIAM model. These drivers are described in Section 1.5.2: Introduction to SIAM.

2.1.3. Inputs

Inputs to this stage include:

- Enterprise, corporate, and IT governance standards
- Current business, procurement and IT strategies
- Business requirements and constraints
- Current organization structure, processes, products and practices
- Existing service provider information, including existing contracts and agreements
- Understanding of market forces and technology trends.

2.1.4. Activities

The activities in this stage are:
1. Establish the project
2. Define strategic objectives
3. Define governance requirements and the high-level governance framework
4. Define principles and policies for roles and responsibilities
5. Map the existing services and sourcing environment
6. Assess the organization's current maturity and capability
7. Understand the marketplace
8. Define the strategy for SIAM and the outline SIAM model
9. Produce the outline business case.

2.1.4.1. Activity: Establish the Project

The SIAM transformation project should be formally established using the organization's selected project management methodology.

This includes:
- Setting up a project management office
- Defining roles and responsibilities for the project
- Setting up project governance
- Agreeing the approach for managing project risks.

The organization will also choose whether to carry out a waterfall project or use an Agile project management approach.

2.1.4.2. Activity: Define the Strategic Objectives

Strategic objectives are the long-term goals of the organization that SIAM is intended to support.

They are related to the drivers for SIAM and the SIAM business case. The objectives defined and agreed in this activity will be used as a basis for items including the:
- SIAM model
- SIAM governance framework
- Sourcing model
- Roles and responsibilities.

2.1.4.3. Activity: Define the Governance Requirements and High-level Governance Framework

SIAM requires a specific governance framework that allows the customer organization to exercise and maintain authority over the SIAM ecosystem.

The model should be tailored to the specific SIAM structures, the SIAM model, and the customer organization's overall appetite for risk.

At this stage, the SIAM governance framework will be defined at a high-level. It should include:
- Specific corporate governance requirements that support any external regulations and legal requirements
- Controls to be retained and operated by customer organization
- Definition of governance boards and governance board structures
- Segregation of duties between the customer organization and external organizations
- Risk management approach
- Performance management approach
- Contract management approach
- Dispute management approach.

2.1.4.4. Activity: Define Principles and Policies for Roles and Responsibilities

In this activity, the key principles and policies for roles and responsibilities are created. They will take into account the governance requirements and strategic objectives.

The specific, detailed roles and responsibilities will not be defined or assigned until more detailed process models and sourcing agreements have been designed within the Plan and Build stage.

Two aspects should be considered here:
- Segregation of duties if one organization is operating in more than one SIAM layer
- Boundaries of delegated authority.

2.1.4.5.   Activity: Map the Existing Services and Sourcing Environment

Before a SIAM model can be designed, the current environment must be understood. This includes:
- Existing services and the service hierarchy
- Existing service providers (internal and external)
- Contracts
- Service provider performance
- Relationships with service providers
- Cost of services.

The creation of the service hierarchy is a critical activity to support the design of the desired future state. The hierarchy enables the identification of essential business functions, critical service assets and dependencies across the ecosystem.

This activity will provide clarity on the current environment. It can also help to highlight issues including:
- Duplications in service offerings
- Misaligned contractual commitments
- Unused operational services
- Uneconomic services
- Service risks that require mitigation.

Information about service providers can be used to decide whether they are to be retained in the current format, or whether their services should be sourced under new arrangements.

2.1.4.6. Activity: Assess Current Maturity and Capability

> Capability *"The power or ability to do something"*[7]
>
> Maturity relates to the degree of formality and optimization of processes, from ad hoc practices, to formally defined steps, to managed result metrics, to active optimization of the processes.[8]
>
> Both capability and maturity need to be assessed to inform the strategy for SIAM.
>
> **For example:** a customer organization may currently have low maturity in service integration processes, practices, and tools; but have a high capability in these areas. This may influence their preferred SIAM structure, leading them to select an internally sourced service integrator.

A baselining exercise should be carried out to understand the customer organization's current capability and maturity in organization, processes, practices and tools. This will inform the next stage of the roadmap.

This exercise can also identify any issues that require a review of earlier decisions. For example, where there is insufficient capability to run the project management office; or insufficient maturity of the incident management process.

---

[7] Source: Oxford English Dictionary © 2016 Oxford University Press
[8] Capability Maturity Model (CMM)

2.1.4.7. Activity: Understand the Marketplace

It is important at this stage to understand the existence and capabilities of potential external service integrators and service providers. This will inform the strategy for SIAM and the SIAM model.

This activity should include a review of available technologies and services against the strategic objectives.

For example, a move to cloud services can support a strategic objective for reduced cost of ownership.

The service providers of commodity cloud services are unlikely to take part in the SIAM model's boards, process forums and working groups. This could reduce the workload of the service integrator, to a level where an internally sourced service integrator may offer better value than an externally sourced service integrator.

2.1.4.8. Activity: Define the Strategy for SIAM and the Outline SIAM Model

This activity will take the information and outputs from previous activities in this stage to define the strategy for SIAM, and an outline SIAM model.

These should include:

Strategy for SIAM
- The vision for SIAM
- Strategic objectives
- Current maturity and capability
- Existing services and sourcing environment
- Marketplace analysis
- Governance requirements
- Proposed SIAM structure, including retained capabilities
- Proposed sourcing approach
- Justification for proposals.

Outline SIAM Model
- Principles and policies
- Governance framework
- Outline roles and responsibilities
- Outline of process models, practices, and structural elements

- Outline of services
- Service providers to be retired.

The strategy for SIAM and the chosen SIAM model both need to align with the original business requirements and the business strategy.

2.1.4.9. Activity: Produce the Outline Business Case

This activity will take the information and outputs from all previous activities in this stage to produce an outline business case for SIAM.

This should include:
- Strategy for SIAM
- Outline SIAM model
- Current state
- Expected benefits from SIAM
- Risks
- Outline costs of the transition to SIAM
- High-level plan.

The outline business case should be approved in accordance with the customer organization's governance arrangements before the next roadmap stage begins.

2.1.5. Outputs

The outputs from the Discovery and Strategy stage are:
1. An established SIAM transition project
2. Strategic objectives
3. Governance requirements and high-level SIAM governance framework
4. Defined principles and policies for roles and responsibilities
5. Map of existing services and sourcing environment
6. Current maturity and capability levels
7. Market awareness
8. Approved outline business case for SIAM
9. Strategy for SIAM
10. Outline SIAM model.

2.2. Plan and Build

2.2.1. Objectives

The Plan and Build stage builds on the outputs from the Discovery and Strategy stage to complete the design for SIAM and create the plans for the transformation.

During this stage, all plans and approvals are put in place before the Implement stage begins. The main objectives for this stage are to:
1. Complete the design of the SIAM model, including the services that are in scope
2. Obtain full approval for the SIAM model
3. Appoint the service integrator and service providers
4. Commence organizational change management.

2.2.2. Triggers

This stage is triggered on completion of the Discovery and Strategy stage, when the organization confirms its intention to proceed with a SIAM implementation.

2.2.3. Inputs

The inputs to this stage are the outline business case, and the high-level model and frameworks created during the Discovery and Strategy stage:

- Governance requirements and high-level SIAM governance framework
- Defined principles and policies for roles and responsibilities
- Map of existing services and sourcing environment
- Current maturity and capability levels
- Market awareness
- Approved outline business case for SIAM
- Strategy for SIAM
- Outline SIAM model.

In this stage, work will be carried out to further define, refine, and add detail to the outputs from the previous stage. Some organizations may choose to use an Agile approach for this.

2.2.4. Activities
The activities during this stage are:
1. Design the detailed SIAM model
2. Approve the full business case
3. Commence organizational change management
4. Appoint the service integrator
5. Appoint service providers
6. Plan for service provider and service retirement
7. Review stage and approve implementation.

2.2.4.1.   Activity: Design the Detailed SIAM Model

The SIAM model provides the detail for how SIAM will be applied across all parties in the SIAM ecosystem. It contains many elements, including:
1. Service model and sourcing approach
2. The selected SIAM structure
3. Process models
4. Governance model
5. Detailed roles and responsibilities
6. Performance management and reporting framework
7. Collaboration model
8. Tooling strategy
9. Ongoing improvement framework.

Careful design of this model is critical to success. The design activities will not necessarily be sequential. There is more likely to be an iterative cycle, which starts with an initial definition, and becomes successively more detailed as each iteration is agreed.

There must be regular review and feedback across all the design activities. Agile approaches can be particularly useful for this. Consideration must also be given to interdependencies between the different design activities.

Organizations will determine the level of detail they require for their own SIAM model. This will depend on several factors, including:
- Strategic objectives
- Market conditions
- Services and service complexity
- Number of service providers
- Appetite for risk
- Resource and process capability and maturity

- Available tools
- Budget.

2.2.4.1.1. Define Service Model and Sourcing Approach

This activity defines the services in scope for the SIAM model, the service hierarchy, and how the services are grouped for sourcing. Creating the service model is a critical activity for an effective transition to SIAM.

These areas must be clearly defined for each service:
- The service provider(s)
- The service consumer(s)
- The service characteristics, including service levels
- The service boundaries
- Dependencies with other services
- Technical interactions with other services
- Data and information interactions with other services
- Service outcomes, value, and objectives.

Services should be placed into groups, with groups assigned to specific service providers. The service model shows the hierarchy of the proposed services, and the service provider for each service. This forms part of the overall SIAM model.

The model should also include the expected process interactions between the services and service providers. Enabling practices like OBASHI[9] can support this by mapping dataflow between service providers.

The service model will help to identify omissions, single points of failure, and duplication.

The aim should be to achieve a balance between getting 'best of breed' services, the number of services and service providers, and the complexity of the service model and hierarchy. There also needs to be a balance between service complexity and integration complexity. Services should be designed to minimize interactions with other services, as these interactions drive complexity, risk, and cost.

---

[9] See OBASHI.co.uk for further information

Care should be taken when defining the services and assigning them to service providers. The number of contact points, interactions, and therefore opportunities for failure, will increase as the number of services and service providers increase.

Sourcing Approach for Services
The ability to source services in groups is one of the benefits of SIAM. Rather than having a single, monolithic contract with one service provider delivering everything, the full range of services can be broken down into the most efficient and best value groupings. Each group is then individually sourced, externally or internally.

Common examples of service groups include:
1. Hosting
2. Application development and support
3. Desktop support/end user computing
4. Networks
5. Cloud services
6. Managed services.

Each group can be provided by one or more service providers. For example, a 'hosting' group could include Platform as a Service (PaaS) and Infrastructure as a Service (IaaS), sourced from one or multiple providers.

The design of service groups should try to minimize any technical dependencies between services. Dependencies create interactions between service providers and potential points of failure, and can increase the workload of the service integrator.

There is no requirement within the SIAM management methodology to separate services that logically stay together. For example, there is no need to divide a Software as a Service offering into 'hosting' and 'application development and support' if it is more logical to source it as one group.

Unnecessary separation can cause issues, such as disputes about who is responsible for performance problems. This particularly applies to managed services, legacy services, cloud services, and DevOps services.

There is no limit to the number of different groups within a SIAM model. However, integration complexity will increase as the number of service groups increases.

2.2.4.1.2. Select the SIAM Structure

The selected SIAM structure determines the sourcing approach for the service integrator. This is a crucial decision that must be taken with care, as any changes to the structure after this point will result in re-work and cost.

All the information gathered so far should be used to select the preferred SIAM structure. If this is different from the proposal created during the Discovery and Strategy stage, it may be necessary to repeat parts of that stage.

See Section 3: SIAM Structures for more information on the advantages and disadvantages of each structure.

2.2.4.1.3. Design Process Models

In a SIAM model, the execution of most processes will involve multiple service providers. Each service provider might carry out individual steps in a different way, but as part of an overall integrated process model.

Process models are therefore important SIAM artefacts; the individual processes and work instructions are likely to remain within the domain of the individual providers.

The process model for each process should describe:
- Purpose and outcomes
- High-level activities
- Inputs, outputs, interactions and dependencies with other processes
- Inputs, outputs, and interactions between the different parties (for example, between the service providers and the service integrator)
- Controls
- Measures
- Supporting policies and templates.

Techniques such as swim lane models, RACI matrices, and process mapping are commonly used and are helpful for establishing and communicating process models.

The process models will continue to evolve and improve as further activities are undertaken in this stage, and in the Run and Improve stage. This includes getting input from the selected service providers and service integrator.

> **Adding Granularity**
>
> The iterative design and development of the SIAM structure, services and service groups, roles and responsibilities, governance model, process models, performance management and reporting framework, collaboration model, tooling strategy and ongoing improvement framework, all add detail to the SIAM model.
>
> This detailed work and iterative approach is critical to ensure that the SIAM model will work once implemented, and that it aligns with the strategy for SIAM and the customer organization's requirements.

2.2.4.1.4. Design Governance Model

The governance model should be designed using the governance framework and the roles and responsibilities. For each governance body, this model should include:

- Scope
- Accountabilities
- Responsibilities
- Meeting formats
- Meeting frequencies
- Inputs
- Outputs (including reports)
- Hierarchy
- Terms of reference
- Related policies.

The governance framework should also be updated and more detail added. This is an iterative activity that should be completed before the end of this roadmap stage.

2.2.4.1.5. Design Roles and Responsibilities

Roles and responsibilities should be designed using the outline SIAM model and outline process models, the SIAM structure and the governance framework.

This should include the detailed design and allocation of roles and responsibilities to:
- Process models
- Practices
- Governance boards
- Process forums
- Working groups
- Organizational structures and locations for any retained capabilities.

This work may highlight a need to review earlier designs and decisions.

Roles and responsibilities can be further developed in the Run and Improve stage, but the detail must be confirmed in this stage before any service integrator or service providers can be appointed.

2.2.4.1.6. Design Performance Management and Reporting Framework

The performance management and reporting framework for SIAM addresses measuring and reporting on a range of items including:
- Key performance indicators
- Performance of processes and process models
- Achievement of service level targets
- System and service performance
- Adherence to contractual and non-contractual responsibilities
- Collaboration
- Customer satisfaction.

Measurements should be taken for each service provider and its services, but also across the end to end SIAM ecosystem.

Designing an appropriate performance management and reporting framework for a SIAM ecosystem can be challenging. It is usually straightforward to measure the performance of an individual service provider; the challenge is in measuring end to end performance as experienced by the users, particularly when there may be limited consistency in how each of the providers measure and report.

The framework should also include the standards for:
- Data classification
- Reporting formats and frequency.

2.2.4.1.7. Design Collaboration Model

SIAM can only be effective when service providers, the service integrator and the customer can communicate and collaborate with each other.

Section 7: SIAM Cultural Considerations has some examples of how to encourage collaboration in SIAM ecosystems.

2.2.4.1.8. Define Tooling Strategy

A consistent and comprehensive tooling strategy is important within a SIAM ecosystem. The tooling strategy is influenced by:
- The selected SIAM structure
- The SIAM model
- Existing customer toolsets
- Service provider and service integrator toolsets
- Types of service provider
- Budget.

The tooling strategy should focus on supporting the flow of data and information and process integration efficiently:
- Between the service providers
- Between service providers and the service integrator
- Between the service integrator and the customer.

This is more important than focusing on technology alone.

Many organizations use more than one toolset in their SIAM ecosystem, selecting a range of 'best of breed' toolsets for:
- Supporting service management processes
- Data analysis
- Reporting and presentation
- Event monitoring
- Audit logging.

There are four main options for toolsets:
1. A single toolset is used by all parties, mandated by the customer
2. The service providers use their own toolsets and integrate them with the service integrator's toolset
3. The service providers use their own toolsets and the service integrator integrates them with its own toolset
4. An integration service is used to integrate the toolsets of the service providers and the service integrator.

The tooling strategy should include:
- Enterprise architecture
- Functional and non-functional requirements
- Integration requirements (technical and logical)
- Data mapping for each SIAM layer
- Data ownership
- Access control
- Measurement and reporting.

2.2.4.1.9. Design Ongoing Improvement Framework

An improvement framework needs to be developed and maintained in conjunction with all parties within the SIAM model. This will ensure a focus on continual improvement across the SIAM ecosystem.

Service providers should have incentives that encourage them to suggest and deliver improvements and innovation.

2.2.4.2. Activity: Approve Full Business Case

At this point, the design should be detailed and complete enough to enable the full costs of the SIAM transition and the anticipated benefits to be determined.

The outline business case should be reviewed and updated with detailed information to create a full business case.

This should then be approved using the organization's corporate governance and approvals process. The approval allows the start of procurement activities for any external service providers, service integrator, and tools.

2.2.4.3. Activity: Commence Organizational Change Management

A SIAM transformation is a major business change, affecting the customer organization, service integrator and service providers at every level.

Organizational change management will be essential if the transformation is to succeed.

During any organizational change, it is important to protect the existing service and minimize the impact on the existing organization.

2.2.4.4. Activity: Appoint the Service Integrator

Ideally, the service integrator should be selected and in place before the SIAM model is finalised and before any service providers are selected.

If this can be achieved, the service integrator can be involved with the Plan and Build activities. The benefits of this approach are:

- The service integrator is involved with the design and selection of service providers, so it can use its experience to assist with these activities
- The service integrator is fully aware of the requirements placed on the service providers during selection and appointment.

The selection process and contractual agreement for an external service integrator may take some time. On occasion, the customer might source the service integrator and the service providers simultaneously.

Alternatively, the service providers might already be in place or undergoing transition from legacy contracts before the service integrator role is confirmed.

2.2.4.5. Activity: Appoint Service Providers

Service providers cannot be selected until this point, as it will not be possible to fully document the requirements until the SIAM model has been fully defined.

The contracts in place in a SIAM model need to support the overall strategy for SIAM. It is important to ensure that they include appropriate targets and risk and reward models. Detailed requirements should be included in any contracts or internal agreements.

> **Cloud Services**
>
> Where cloud services have been selected, requirements often need to be adjusted to consider that these are commodity services.
>
> For example, cloud commodity service providers are unlikely to take part in boards, process forums or working groups, to change their processes, or to integrate their toolsets with others.

The challenge is to balance the customer's desire for specific requirements against what is offered in the marketplace. Forcing service providers to customize their delivery models can result in increased costs and risks.

The procurement of external service providers can take some time, which needs to be included in any plan or timeline.

It is important to verify that the desired service providers can meet the full set of requirements in the SIAM model, particularly for strategic service providers. If there are issues or gaps, this may require a return to earlier lifecycle stages and activities.

In addition to the service providers that are appointed here, it is important to remember that service providers can be added and removed throughout the SIAM roadmap. Some service providers may not be appointed until after a legacy contract has expired.

2.2.4.6. Activity: Plan for Service Provider and Service Retirement

Planning also needs to address retiring services, and any resulting transfer of services to new service providers.

The relationships with any service providers, service dependencies, contract end dates and potential impact of retiring a particular service or service provider must be carefully considered.

Detailed plans should be developed for any decommissioning, discontinuation, and transfer of services. The plans need to include contractual restrictions, legal requirements, and lead times for service termination.

They must also detail how data, information, and knowledge will be transferred from retiring service providers, including:
- What needs to be transferred
- To whom it will be transferred
- When it needs to be transferred
- How to assess if the transfer is successful.

See SIAM 8: SIAM Challenges and Risks for more information about legacy contracts.

2.2.4.7. Activity: Review Stage and Approve Implementation

The outputs from this stage should be reviewed against decisions taken in the previous stage, to identify if there are any issues or necessary changes. The roadmap will then progress on to the Implement stage if approval is given.

2.2.5. Outputs

The outputs from the Plan and Build stage are:
- Full design of the SIAM model including:
    - Services, service groups, and service providers (the 'service model')
    - The selected SIAM structure
    - Process models
    - Practices
    - Structural elements
    - Roles and responsibilities
    - Governance model
    - Performance management and reporting framework
    - Collaboration model
    - Tooling strategy
    - Ongoing improvement framework
- Approved business case
- Organizational change management activities
- Service integrator appointed
- Service providers appointed
- Plan for service provider and service retirement.

There may be several iterations during this stage before the outputs are complete and the roadmap progresses to the next stage.

The outputs from Plan and Build must be detailed enough to support the implementation activities.

2.3. Implement

2.3.1. Objectives

The objective of this stage is to manage the transition from the organization's 'as is' current state to the 'to be' desired future state, the new SIAM model. At the end of this stage, the new SIAM model will be in place and in use.

2.3.2. Triggers

This stage is triggered when the organization completes all activities of the Strategy and Design and Plan and Build stages.

The timing for the start of the Implement stage can be influenced by events in the existing environment. For example, implementation could be triggered by:
- The end of an existing service provider's contract
- An existing service provider ceasing to trade
- Organizational structure changes due to corporate restructure or takeover.

The customer organization may have limited control over the timing of these events. It may need to react to them by completing as many of the Discovery, Strategy, Plan and Build activities as possible. There will be an increased level of risk if the activities from these stages are not fully completed owing to a lack of time.

2.3.3. Inputs

All the outputs from the Discovery and Strategy and Plan and Build stages form inputs for the Implement stage.

2.3.4. Activities
The activities in this stage focus on making the transition to the new SIAM model. They include:
1. Select the implementation approach
2. Transition to the approved SIAM model
3. Ongoing organizational change management.

2.3.4.1. Activity: Selecting the Implementation Approach
There are two possible approaches to implementation:
1. 'Big bang'
2. Phased.

2.3.4.1.1. 'Big Bang' Implementation
A 'big bang' implementation approach is one that introduces everything at once, including: the service integrator, the service providers (with new contracts) and the new ways of working.

The 'big bang' approach can be high risk, because it affects the entire organization at the same time. The resulting impact on the customer's business and the services provided can be very high, unless the risks are planned for and carefully managed.

Most organizations who adopt SIAM are introducing it into an environment with existing providers, contracts and relationships. This can mean that 'big bang' is not possible, as different contracts expire at different times. The 'big bang' approach does provide an opportunity to make a 'clean break' from all legacy issues and behaviours at the same time and avoids the complexities of managing a phased approach.

2.3.4.1.2. Phased Implementation
A phased implementation approach makes the transformation to the new SIAM model in smaller, more easily managed transition projects and iterations. This can be achieved in several ways, including:
- One service at a time
- One service provider at a time
- One practice at a time
- One process at a time.

This phased approach to SIAM implementation can lower the level of risk associated with the transition, but can be more complex to manage and will extend the total time for implementation. Specific care needs to be given to define and understand the impact of each transition and to ensure that the delivery of existing services continues with no disruption.

2.3.4.2. Activity: Transition to the Approved SIAM Model

The transition activities will be dependent on the selected approach; phased or 'big bang'.

This activity involves:
- Establishing processes and supporting infrastructure
- Commencing transition activity to new service providers and services
- Removing service providers who are not part of the SIAM model
- Verifying the successful execution of the transition steps
- Toolset and process alignment between all parties.

This is not a trivial activity. The number of service providers, services, processes and toolsets will all affect the complexity of the transition. It involves the transition to the full SIAM model, including the implementation of new:
- Service providers
- Services
- Service integrator
- Process models
- Roles and responsibilities
- Tools
- Practices
- Structural elements
- Contracts and agreements
- Governance framework
- Performance management and reporting framework.

A robust methodology should be used for this transition, including:
- Testing (both functional and non-functional)
- Data migration
- Service introduction
- Deployment testing
- Service acceptance
- Post-transition support.

The transition normally requires resources who are specifically dedicated to and focused on it.

The service providers selected during Plan and Build will need to be transferred into the SIAM ecosystem as part of the Implement stage.

Existing service providers who are taking on a new role in the SIAM ecosystem will need to fully understand their new role, relationships and interfaces. New service providers will need to be transitioned into the ecosystem in a managed way.

This activity should be managed by the service integrator on behalf of the customer. It is vital that clear ownership and roles and responsibilities are agreed, including reporting lines, escalation paths and mandates to ensure efficient and effective decision making.

2.3.4.3. Activity: Ongoing Organizational Change Management

Organizational change management started in the Plan and Build stage of the roadmap. It continues through this stage and into the next.

Specific activities in the Implement stage include:
- Conducting awareness campaigns throughout the organization
- Communicating with and preparing stakeholders for the change
- Ensuring appropriate training is completed
- Continuing with deployment of the organizational change plans
- Measurement of the effectiveness of communications and organizational change activities.

It is important to focus on protecting the existing service and minimizing organizational impact during this stage.

2.3.5. Outputs
The output from the Implement stage is the new SIAM model that is in place and operating, and supported by appropriate contracts and agreements.

2.4. Run and Improve

2.4.1. Objectives
The objectives of the Run and Improve stage include:
- Manage the SIAM model
- Manage day to day service delivery
- Manage processes, teams and tools
- Manage the continual improvement activities.

2.4.2. Triggers
This stage is triggered when the Implement stage is completed. If the chosen implementation approach is 'phased', Run and Improve will take over elements of delivery in an incremental way, as each phase, service, process or service provider exits the Implement stage.

2.4.3. Inputs
Inputs to this stage will include:
- The SIAM model
- Process models
- Performance management and reporting framework
- Collaboration model for providers
- Tooling strategy
- Ongoing improvement framework.

These inputs have been designed during the Discovery and Strategy and Plan and Build stages, and then transferred during the Implement stage.

2.4.4. Activities

The activities in this stage focus on providing consistent, guaranteed service outcomes to the business, which can be managed, measured and improved. They include:
1. Operate governance structural elements
2. Performance management and improvement
3. Operate management structural elements
4. Audit and compliance
5. Reward
6. Ongoing change management.

> In the Run and Improve stage, the new operating model should no longer be seen as 'new'; it is just how things are done.

2.4.4.1. Activity: Operate Governance Structural Elements

Governance boards provide an important role in the control of the overall SIAM ecosystem.

During the Plan and Build stage, the high-level governance framework was created. In Implement, it was transferred to the live environment. In Run and Improve, governance board members adopt their new roles.

See Section 5: SIAM Roles and Responsibilities and Section 1: Introduction to SIAM for more information about governance boards.

2.4.4.2. Activity: Performance Management and Improvement

The performance of all services and processes should be measured and monitored against key performance indicators and, where appropriate, service level targets. The measurements should be both qualitative and quantitative.

Measurements are used to create meaningful and understandable reports for the appropriate audiences. They provide visibility of performance issues, and support trend analysis to give early warning of possible failures.

Routine service improvement activities should include review and management of actions arising from the information and review of report relevance.

Within SIAM, reports also need to include feedback for how the service is perceived by users, referred to as qualitative reporting. For more information, see Section 6: SIAM practices.

Reports can be used to identify opportunities for improvement and innovation.

2.4.4.3. Activity: Operate Management Structural Elements

Process forums and working groups are two of the structural elements that unite the service integrator, service providers and the customer.

They provide an environment to work collaboratively on the operation of a specific process or processes, process outputs, issue or project.

In this stage of the roadmap, these forums and groups should be actively working. The frequency and format of meetings will vary, but it is a good idea to have regular contact between the forum and group members in the early stages of implementation, as they will be instrumental in creating the necessary collaborative culture.

See Section 5: SIAM Roles and Responsibilities, Section 7: SIAM Culture, and Section 1: Introduction to SIAM for more information about process forums and working groups.

2.4.4.4. Activity: Audit and Compliance

In addition to the review of reports that takes place in a SIAM environment, a more formal audit schedule should also be introduced.

This can include process audits, service audits, service provider audits; whatever is most appropriate for each organization and the SIAM ecosystem.
Some audits will be mandated by regulations, legislation or corporate governance.

These audits may be performed by an external organization.
Audits support ongoing assurance of compliance to the customer organization's legislative and regulatory requirements. They can provide valuable information about whether elements of the model are working as they should and help to embed a culture of improvement.

2.4.4.5. Activity: Reward

A SIAM ecosystem can challenge all stakeholders to behave in new ways. Service providers must be encouraged to collaborate rather than protect their own interests. Reward mechanisms can be used to encourage collaboration and communication.

Good practices for creating a reward system include:
- Use small rewards often, linked to specific actions
- Give rewards at unexpected times
- Reward the behaviour, not just the results
- Reward all stakeholders, not just one layer of the SIAM model
- Reward publicly.

> **Case Study**
> One customer organization has created a CIO Award for Collaboration.
>
> This is given quarterly to the service provider who has demonstrated excellent behaviours, including collaboration, willingness to help others, and ease of working with them. The scores are collated and shared with all parties.
>
> Crucially, service providers are encouraged to nominate each other, encouraging them to recognize good behaviour within the service provider layer.

2.4.4.6. Activity: Ongoing Change Management

After the SIAM model enters the Run and Improve stage, it will change and evolve as the sourcing landscape and business requirements change and evolve.

Ongoing change management will include the addition and removal of service providers, scaling the services if customer needs get grow or shrink, and potentially changing the SIAM structure.

If major change is required, this can include going back to earlier roadmap stages, for example to revisit Discovery and Strategy.

2.4.5. Outputs
Outputs from the Run and Improve stage fall into two categories:
- Run outputs: business as usual outputs including reports, service data and process data
- Improve outputs: information used to evolve and continually improve the SIAM model.

3. SIAM Structures

There are four common structures for a SIAM ecosystem. The difference between each structure is the sourcing and configuration of the service integrator layer.

The structures are:
- Externally sourced
- Internally sourced
- Hybrid
- Lead supplier.

The customer organization will choose a structure based on factors including:
- Business requirements
- Internal capabilities (including maturity, resources and skills)
- Complexity of the customer's services
- Customer's organizational structure and size
- Legislative and regulatory environment
- Customer budget
- Current organizational maturity and capability in service integration and IT
- Appetite for external sourcing/loss of direct control
- Required timescales
- Appetite for risk
- Types and numbers of service providers to be managed.

3.1. Externally Sourced Service Integrator

In this structure, the customer appoints an external organization to take the role and provide the capabilities of the service integrator.

The service provider roles are performed by external service providers and/or internal service providers.

The externally sourced service integrator is exclusively focused on service integration activities and does not take any of the service provider roles, as illustrated in figure 9.

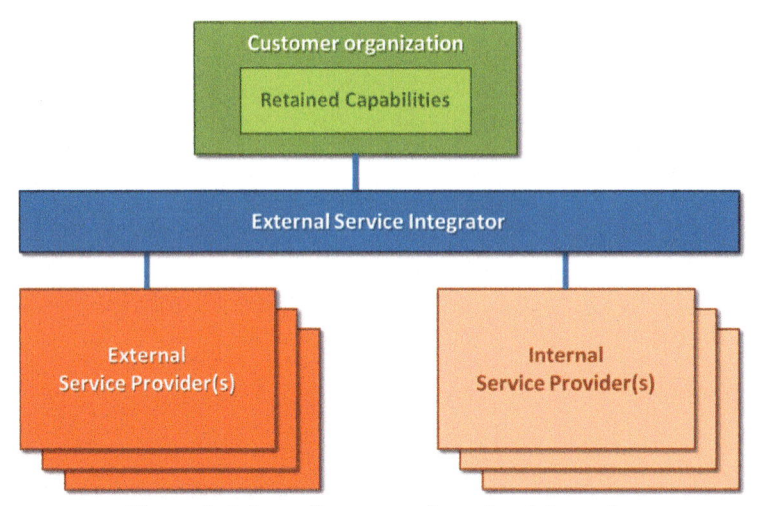

Figure 9. Externally sourced service integrator

3.1.1. When does a Customer use this Structure?

This structure is suitable when the customer organization does not have in-house service integration capabilities and does not intend to develop them.

It is also commonly chosen by organizations who do not have the resources available to take on the service integrator role, and do not want to have an increased headcount or the management responsibilities associated with selecting and maintaining service integration resources.

This structure is suitable for customers who are prepared for another organization to take the service integrator role, and who are prepared to have a high degree of trust in their external service integrator.

It relies on the customer empowering the service integrator and giving it the responsibilities of day-to-day coordination and control of service providers, implementing and coordinating processes and managing end to end reporting.

For this structure to succeed, the customer needs retained capabilities to provide strong governance over the external service integrator. These capabilities will identify the goals and the mandate for the external service integrator, and will communicate them clearly to all stakeholders.

The customer must allow the service integrator to act on its behalf. The customer should not bypass the service integrator by having direct operational relationships with the service providers.

> **Summary: Externally Sourced**
>
> Suitable for:
> - Customers who are prepared for another organization to take the service integrator role
> - Customers who are prepared to have a high degree of trust in an external organization acting as their service integrator
> - Customers who do not have service integration capabilities and do not want to develop them
> - Customers who do not have service integration resources and do not want to add or manage them.

3.1.2. Advantages

The advantages of an externally sourced service integrator include:
- The opportunity for the customer to review multiple service integrators and then select an experienced service integrator with good reviews from previous clients
- The potential for faster benefits realization, as the service integrator's expertise reduces the time to implement the SIAM roadmap; although the time required to select the external service integrator also needs to be considered
- The potential for improved value, as the service integrator applies its experience to manage the SIAM ecosystem in an efficient and effective way
- Separation of concerns: the service integrator can focus on the end to end governance and coordination of the service, processes, metrics and reporting and the customer

organization can focus on business outcomes and strategic objectives
- Access to established SIAM models, processes and toolsets, where the service integrator is providing the toolset
- Access to innovative practices from the service integrator's experience on other SIAM implementations.

3.1.3. Disadvantages

The disadvantages of an externally sourced service integrator include:
- The high-level of dependency on the external service integrator adds a level of risk; including commercial, continuity and security risks
- The potential for higher costs related to the sourcing and management of an external organization
- The potential for resentment from any internal service provider that is part of the customer organization, but is being managed by an external organization
- The potential for resentment from the external service providers in the SIAM ecosystem, particularly where the service providers and service integrator compete in other markets. This can lead to relationship issues and poor performance
- The external service integrator's models and practices might not be the best fit for the customer organization
- The use of an external service integrator can make it more difficult to change how the service integrator is working, because contractual changes may be required. This means the customer will be less agile and may result in higher costs
- There is a risk that the customer decides to appoint an external service integrator because they do not fully understand SIAM themselves. This is likely to increase overall costs of delivery and result in poor service because the customer hasn't clearly defined their own objectives
- The external service integrator must build relationships with the customer organization and with the service providers; the time and effort required to do this if often not accounted for in the initial investment analysis

- The service integrator does not have a contractual relationship with the service providers, so, without empowerment from the customer, they can be ineffective.

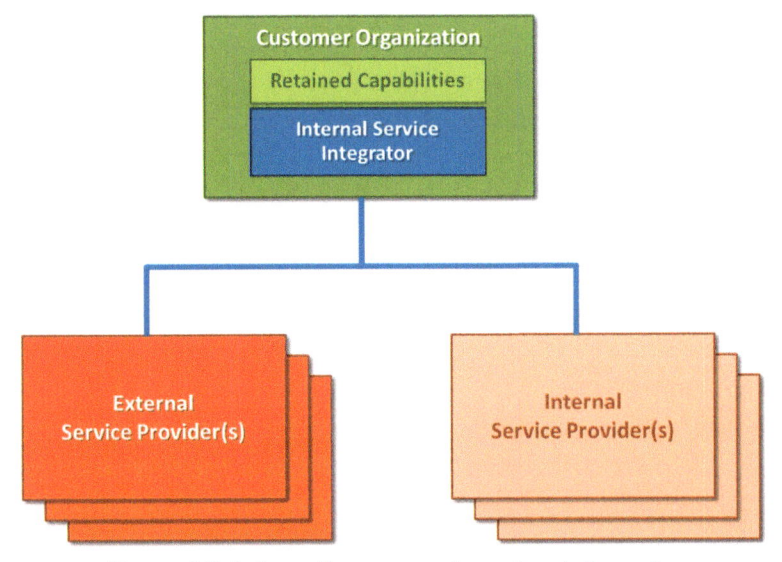

3.2. Internally Sourced Service Integrator

In this SIAM structure, the customer organization takes the role of service integrator, providing the service integration capability. The service integrator role and the customer role still need to be defined and managed separately.

If the customer role and the service integrator role become inseparable and indistinct, service providers may interact with the customer as if it was part of a traditional outsourced ecosystem. The benefits of moving to a SIAM model would not be realized.

The service provider roles are performed by external service providers and/or internal service providers.

The internally sourced service integrator is exclusively focused on service integration activities.

Figure 10 shows the internally sourced service integrator structure.

Figure 10. Internally sourced service integrator

3.2.1. When does a Customer use this Structure?

This structure is suitable for organizations where the customer already has or intends to develop in-house service integration capabilities.

It is typically used where the customer wants to retain control and flexibility over the SIAM ecosystem, or where timescales do not facilitate the procurement and establishment of an external service integrator. It is also used by organizations that have a business, regulatory or legislative need to retain ownership of the service integration layer.

As part of this structure, the customer may use resource augmentation. This is an approach where many of the individual roles within the service integrator are filled using directly employed internal staff, supplemented by resources provided by an external organization. Even though some of the staff might not be directly employed by the customer, this still fulfils the criteria for an internally sourced service integrator as the customer has overall ownership and control.

> **Summary: Internally Sourced**
>
> Suitable for:
> - Customers who have in-house service integration capabilities or plan to develop them
> - Customers who have business, regulatory or legislative requirements relating to the governance and management of service providers
> - Customers who want to retain control and flexibility over the SIAM ecosystem
> - Customers whose timescales do not allow procurement of an external service integrator.

3.2.2. Advantages

The advantages of an internally sourced service integrator include:
- The customer has full control over the service integrator role, with no dependency on an external company, or any of the associated risks and costs
- Valuable skills remain in-house and there is no loss of key resources or key knowledge

- The service integrator shares strategic goals with the customer organization so there is no conflict
- The service integrator can be flexible and accommodate change without a requirement for any contractual amendments
- External service providers will not see the service integrator as a competitor and are thus more likely to cooperate and collaborate with the service integrator
- The service integrator can be established more quickly because it already understands the customer organization's goals and drivers, and as there is no time required to procure and establish an external service integrator
- The service integrator is part of the same organization that manages service provider contracts so has direct leverage over service providers and their behaviour and performance.

3.2.3. Disadvantages

The disadvantages of an internally sourced service integrator include:
- The customer must develop and maintain the service integrator capability, resources and skills, and design and implement toolsets, sometimes with no experience of SIAM implementation
- The customer may underestimate the number of resources and the expertise required for the service integrator capability
- The service integrator is seen as synonymous with the customer organization; this can make it more challenging for them to mediate between the customer and the service providers if there is a conflict
- There is a risk that the customer decides to act as the service integrator because they are not fully committed to SIAM, and do not wish to formally establish and outsource the structure. If SIAM is not adopted fully, the benefits will be limited and there will be a further risk that old ways of working continue
- Internal service providers may not accept the authority of the internal service integrator.

3.3. Hybrid Service Integrator

In this structure, the customer collaborates with an external organization to take the role of service integrator and provide the service integrator capability.

The service provider roles are performed by external service providers and/or internal service providers.

The hybrid service integrator is exclusively focused on service integration activities and does not take any of the service provider roles.

The hybrid service integrator structure is shown in figure 11.

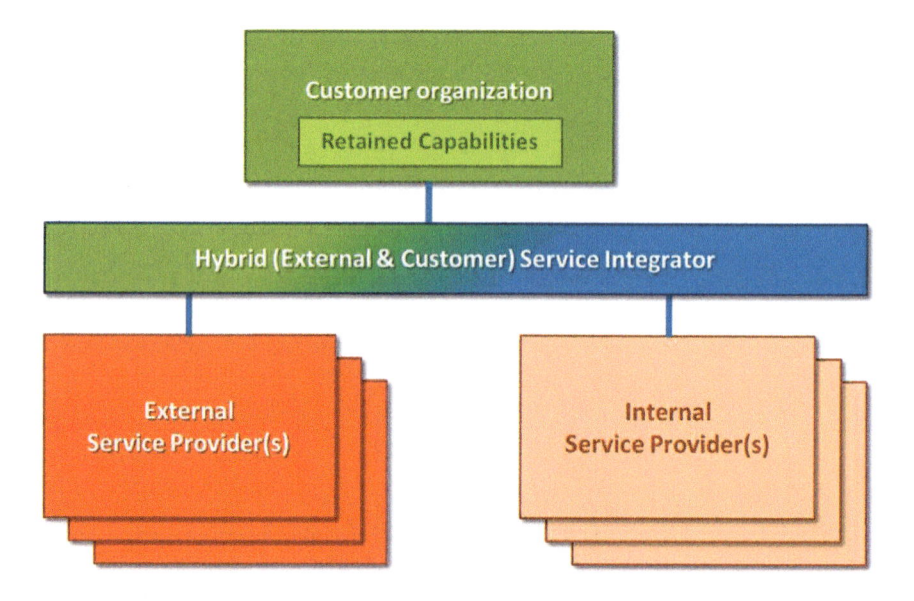

Figure 11 Hybrid service integrator

3.3.1. When does a Customer use this Structure?

This structure is suitable for organizations that wish to retain an element of involvement in the service integrator role, but do not have sufficient in-house capabilities or resources.

In the hybrid structure, the service integration capability is created through collaboration between the customer and an external service integrator acting as a service integration partner. This can allow the customer organization to learn from an external service integrator that already has expertise in that role.

This structure can be temporary or permanent. If it is temporary, the hybrid approach will end when the customer has developed sufficient service integration skills and resources in-house and has moved to an internally sourced structure. If it is permanent, the hybrid approach will continue indefinitely.

In this structure, it is normal to allocate specific service integration roles, functions and structures to either the customer or the service integration partner. This differentiates this structure from the resource augmentation approach that can be applied to the internally sourced structure.

> **Summary: Hybrid**
>
> Suitable for:
> - Customers who want to act as a service integrator but do not have sufficient capability or resources
> - Customers who want to learn from an external service integrator
> - Customers who want the flexibility of a temporary or permanent hybrid service integrator.

3.3.2. Advantages

The advantages of a hybrid service integrator include:
- The customer develops skills and resources, and can revert to an internally sourced solution if the service integration partner fails to live up to initial expectations
- Benefits can be realized more quickly, as the service integrator brings expertise and collaborates with the customer, reducing the time it takes to transition to a SIAM model
- Access to commercial skills and knowledge; the service integrator can help the customer to negotiate with the service providers and avoid common mistakes.

3.3.3. Disadvantages
The disadvantages of a hybrid service integrator include:
- The customer must develop a service integration capability, and recruit and manage resources
- Without clear design, this structure can lead to duplication of skills, missed activities, confusion about responsibilities and poor definition of where the boundaries of operation lie
- This structure can be confusing for the service providers where a clear governance framework and communication plan have not been implemented
- When the hybrid approach is meant to be temporary, the customer may inadvertently build a long-term dependency on the service integration partner
- Organizations may adopt the hybrid model because they are reluctant to give up control, not for a valid business reason. This can lead to the benefits of SIAM not being realized.

3.4. Lead Supplier as Service Integrator

In this structure, the role of service integrator is taken by an external organization that is also an external service provider. This can occur when:
- An existing service provider successfully bids to be the service integrator as part of a procurement process
- The existing service integrator successfully bids to be a service provider as part of a procurement process
- One external organization wins two parts of a tender and so becomes the service integrator and a service provider.

The organization that is a service provider and the service integrator is referred to as the lead supplier.

This structure is sometimes referred to as 'guardian' or 'custodian'. It's important to emphasize that the contractual relationship in this structure remains between the customer organization and the service providers. The service integrator does not have a contractual relationship with the service providers.

Prime Vendor

The lead supplier structure is different to the model known as 'prime' or 'prime vendor', where a service provider sub-contracts other service providers to deliver the service, and the customer only has a contractual relationship with the prime vendor.

Any of the service providers in any of the four SIAM structures could be a prime vendor, using one or more sub-contracted providers as part of its own service delivery. However, these sub-contracts are not visible within the SIAM ecosystem. The relationships in the SIAM ecosystem are between the service provider, the service integrator and the customer. The sub-contracts of a particular service provider are not relevant from the SIAM perspective if the service provider can deliver its service to the agreed levels.

Figure 12 shows the lead supplier structure.

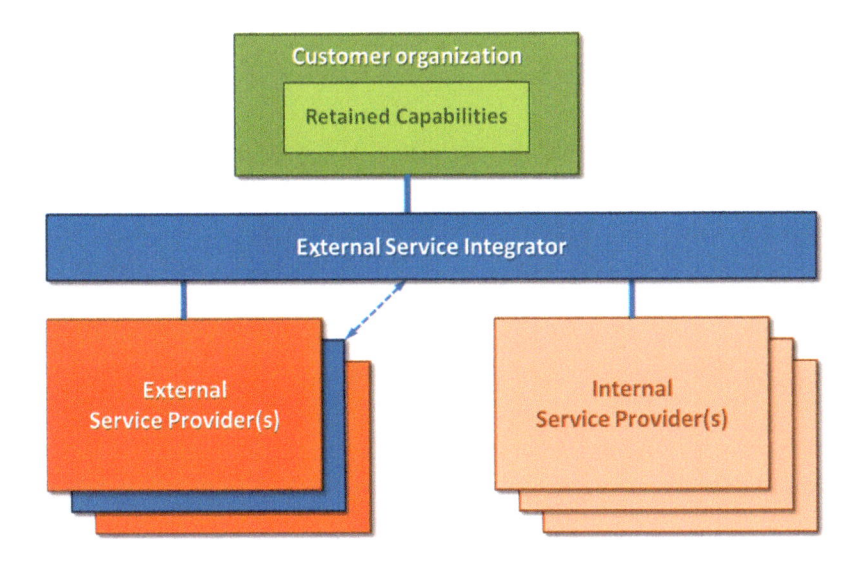

Figure 12 Lead supplier as service integrator

3.4.1. When does a Customer use this Structure?

A customer would choose this structure for the same reasons that it would choose an externally sourced service integrator; i.e. it does not have its own service integration capabilities or resources and does not wish to develop and maintain them.

In this structure, when the customer goes out to tender to choose a service integrator, one of its existing service providers may already have in-depth knowledge of the customer organization, and the customer knows and trusts them. This could facilitate that service provider also being the service integrator.

Conversely, the current service integrator may also have expertise in the delivery of one or more of the services (or service elements) and be could selected for that reason.

If a single organization is acting as both the service integrator and a service provider, there are management considerations that need to be addressed. These include:
- Making sure there is no unfair advantage for the service integrator or the service provider
- Maintaining the impartiality of the service integrator role
- Ensuring that the customer is not being charged twice for the same capabilities.

This requires clear segregation of duties in the lead supplier, often known as 'Chinese walls'.

The service integrator and the service provider roles should be viewed and managed as two separate entities (as if they were separate organizations). They will each have their own contract or agreement, roles, responsibilities and reporting requirements.

Ideally, different resources will work in the service integrator and service provider entities to reduce the likelihood of any conflict of interest.

> **Summary: Lead Supplier**
>
> Suitable for:
> - Customers that have a trusted service provider that also has service integration capabilities
> - Customers that have a trusted service integrator that also has service provider capabilities
> - Customers that are prepared for another organization to take the service integrator role
> - Customers that do not have service integration capabilities or resources and do not plan to develop them.

3.4.2. Advantages

The advantages of a lead supplier service integrator are mostly the same as those for an externally sourced service integrator.

There are some additional advantages:
- Where the service integrator is currently acting as a service provider, the set-up process can be faster as there is an existing relationship with the customer
- From the customer's perspective, the service integrator has a vested interest. If the service fails, it will be subject to penalties at the service provider level, so it has an extra incentive to deliver to agreed targets.

3.4.3. Disadvantages

The disadvantages of a lead supplier service integrator are mostly the same as those for an externally sourced service integrator.

There are some additional disadvantages:
- The organization acting as the service integrator and service provider might not have effective internal governance, leading to knowledge 'leaking' between the two roles. This will create relationship issues between the service integrator and other service providers if this is perceived as an unfair advantage
- The organization acting as the service integrator and service provider might be perceived to be biased, even if this is not

the case, which can also lead to the service integrator/service provider relationships suffering
- The organization acting as service integrator and service provider might charge the customer twice for the same resources; for example, service desk resources shared between the two roles, or management resources shared between the service provider and service integrator roles
- The service integrator part of the organization could treat its service provider function harshly or unfairly to try and prevent any allegations of bias, which can also create relationship and service management issues.

4. SIAM and Other Practices

This section of the Body of Knowledge looks at examples of enabling practices, and how they relate to a SIAM ecosystem.

This includes examples from the management frameworks, methods and standards of:
- IT service management (including ITIL® and ISO/IEC 20000)
- Lean
- COBIT® 5
- DevOps
- Agile, including agile service management.

For each practice, there is a short summary followed by examples of their relevance in a SIAM ecosystem.

This is not an exhaustive list. There are other practices that can complement and support implementation, operation and improvement in a SIAM ecosystem. These include:
- ADKAR: for organizational change
- BiSL: for business information management
- TOGAF, IT4IT, and other architectural practices
- ISO/IEC 30105: for IT enabled services -business process outsourcing
- ISO/IEC 38500: for governance of IT
- CMMI: for services, for process assessments
- OBASHI: for mapping relationships, dependencies, and flows of data and information
- Project management methodologies.

4.1. IT Service Management

IT service management (ITSM) defines the capabilities that support the implementation and management of quality IT services that meet the needs of the business.

IT service management is performed by IT service providers through an appropriate mix of people, process and information technology.

There are two ITSM practices that are particularly relevant to SIAM:
1. ITIL®
2. ISO/IEC 20000.

4.1.1. What is ITIL®?
ITIL® is the most widely accepted approach to IT service management in the world. ITIL® can help individuals and organizations use IT to realize business change, transformation and growth.

ITIL® advocates that IT services are aligned to the needs of the business and support its core processes. It provides guidance to organizations and individuals on how to use IT as a tool to facilitate business change, transformation and growth.

The ITIL® best practices are currently detailed within five core publications:
- Service Strategy
- Service Design
- Service Transition
- Service Operation
- Continual Service Improvement.[10]

These five volumes map the ITIL® service lifecycle.

4.1.2. ITIL in a SIAM Ecosystem
In most cases, transitions to SIAM will take place in an environment that already uses some IT service management processes based on ITIL®.

SIAM doesn't replace ITIL®; it builds on its processes, practices and techniques and adapts them to work effectively in a multi-service provider environment.

Within a SIAM transformation program, consideration must be given to how existing ITIL® processes need to be adapted and augmented to integrate the local processes of multiple service providers.
For example, the incident management process will have similar steps, but will need adaptation to support the transfer of incidents and

---
[10] Source: AXELOS.com

updating of related information between the service providers and with the service integrator.

4.1.2.1. Service Strategy and SIAM

The objective of Service Strategy is to decide on a strategy to serve customers. Starting from an assessment of customer needs and the market place, Service Strategy determines which services the IT organization is to offer and what capabilities need to be developed. Its goal is to make the IT organization think and act in a strategic manner.

Strategic processes include demand management, business relationship management, service portfolio management and financial management.

Within the ITIL® guidance, the customer is accountable and responsible for:
- Setting strategy direction and required outcomes
- Delivery of outcomes
- Execution of strategic processes.

In a SIAM ecosystem:
- The customer is accountable for defining strategy and outcomes
- The accountability for processes to deliver the strategy and outcomes can be devolved to a service integrator
- Service providers are responsible for the delivery of supporting outcomes
- Responsibility for execution of strategic processes may be shared between the customer and the service integrator. For example, the service integrator may collect financial management information which is passed back to the customer for analysis.

4.1.2.2. Service Design and SIAM

The objective of Service Design is to ensure that new and changed services are designed effectively to meet customer expectations.

Design processes include service level management, capacity management, availability management and information security management.

In a SIAM ecosystem, similar processes can be used, but will be adapted to span the SIAM layers:
- The customer is accountable for the overall design and any investment
- The service integrator is accountable for the execution of service design processes for the end to end services. It is also responsible for directing and coordinating the design activities of the service providers
- The service providers are responsible for the execution of the service design processes for their own services, but will need to work with other service providers and the service integrator on the integrated end to end service.

For example, service providers are responsible for capacity management of their own services, but will provide component and system level information and data to the service integrator. The service integrator is then responsible for capacity management of the end to end integrated services, using this data and information. The customer is accountable for taking any strategic investment decisions related to capacity.

4.1.2.3. Service Transition and SIAM

The objective of Service Transition is to build, test, and deploy IT services. Service Transition also makes sure that changes to services and service management processes are carried out in a coordinated way.

Transition processes include change management, release management and configuration management.

Within the SIAM ecosystem:
- The customer is accountable for the approval of strategic changes
- The service integrator is accountable for the successful deployment of changes. It is also responsible for related activities including directing and coordinating the service

providers, assuring integrated changes, and communicating consolidated information on future changes
- The service providers are responsible for the build, test, and deployment of their own changes, and for working with other service providers and the service integrator on the service transition processes for the integrated end to end service.

For example, the service integrator is responsible for an integrated change advisory board which brings together all service providers in the assessment and approval of changes to the end to end services.

4.1.2.4. Service Operation and SIAM

The objective of Service Operation is to ensure that live IT services are delivered effectively and efficiently. This includes fulfilling user requests, resolving service failures, fixing problems, as well as carrying out routine operational tasks.

Operational processes include incident management, problem management, request management and access management. Operational functions include the service desk.

Within the SIAM ecosystem:
- The service integrator is accountable for the successful execution of the service operation processes. It is also responsible for direction and coordination of service providers in circumstances where there is no clear ownership, or when the end to end service levels are compromised
- The service providers are responsible for the execution of the processes, including working with other service providers and the service integrator when their involvement is required.

For example, an incident affecting service availability could be referred to three different service providers for investigation. None of them have identified a possible solution, and the service level is about to be breached. The service integrator needs to step in and manage the situation, coordinating the investigations of the different service providers via a working group.

Each service provider will run their own operational functions, including application management, technical management and IT operations. The service integrator should have a coordinated view of the overall status of service availability, performance, and events. The service provider's supporting processes would provide data to the service integrator.

4.1.2.5. Continual Service Improvement and SIAM

Continual service improvement offers a mechanism for the IT organization to measure and improve service levels, technology and the efficiency and effectiveness of processes used in the overall management of services.

It is important to implement service improvement across the SIAM ecosystem. Getting a single organization to adopt service improvement can be a challenge; the challenge is significantly greater in the layers of the SIAM ecosystem.

The same approaches can be used, but with a focus on a collaborative approach to improvement initiatives. This may require cultural change to support collaboration. See Section 7: SIAM Cultural Considerations for further information.

For example, one service provider wants to introduce new analysis codes to improve problem management trend analysis. Their service is dependent on a service from another service provider. Unless both service providers work together, and with the service integrator, the new analysis codes cannot be introduced.

4.1.3. What is ISO/IEC 20000?

> ISO/IEC 20000 is the first international standard for IT service management. It was developed in 2005... and revised in 2011.
>
> ISO/IEC 20000... was originally developed to reflect best practice guidance contained within the ITIL® framework, although it equally supports other IT service management frameworks and approaches

> including Microsoft Operations Framework and components of
> ISACA's COBIT® framework.[11]

ISO/IEC 20000 is an international standard for IT service management. Organizations can be certified against the standard by an independent Registered Certification Body. It is a standard for IT service providers.

ISO/IEC 20000 requires an organization to have a Service Management System (SMS) that complies with the requirements of the standard. The SMS defines several items including:
- Services, organizations, and locations in scope
- Service management processes
- Service management policies
- Governance of processes operated by other parties.

To obtain certification, organizations must demonstrate compliance with every requirement in the standard, including all processes and policies.

ISO/IEC 20000 includes these process areas:
- Design and transition of new or changed services
- Service delivery
- Resolution
- Relationship
- Control.

Figure 13 shows the process areas and processes in an ISO/IEC 20000 service management system.

---

[11] Source: https://en.wikipedia.org/wiki/ISO/IEC_20000

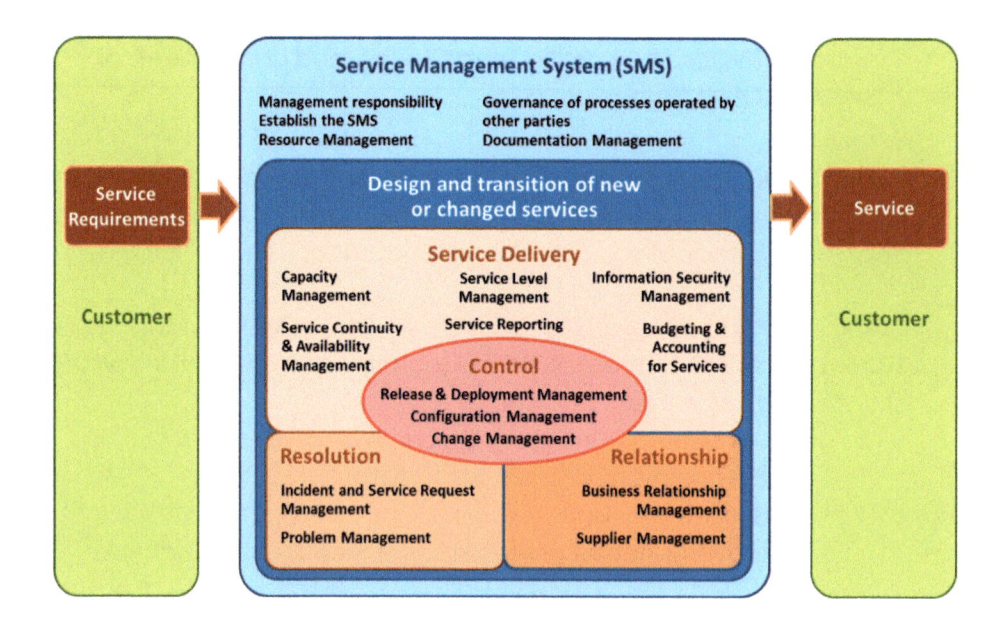

Figure 13 ISO/IEC 20000 service management system

4.1.4. ISO/IEC 20000 in a SIAM Ecosystem

ISO/IEC 20000 is aligned with ITIL®. Most transitions to SIAM will take place in an environment that already uses some IT service management processes that are included in ISO/IEC 20000.

Therefore, it can be useful in SIAM ecosystems, but there are some challenges and limitations that need to be considered. ISO/IEC 20000 was developed from the perspective of IT service providers, not SIAM ecosystems.

Service providers may find the requirements of the standard exclude some essential considerations for SIAM, including:
- Collaboration
- Process integration
- Toolset integration
- Practices
- Multi-organization governance models.

This has been recognized by the standards bodies, and further development of the standard is underway to address these aspects.

The usefulness of the standard in SIAM ecosystems, and the challenges and limitations, are different for each SIAM layer.

4.1.4.1. Customer Layer

Customers who already have ISO/IEC 20000 will need to update their SMS to reflect their transformation to a SIAM ecosystem, and the introduction of a service integrator.

Customers who want to get certification to ISO/IEC 20000 can use their SIAM model as the basis for their SMS. However, getting certification may be a challenge if the service integrator is external, and majority or all the service providers are external.

4.1.4.2. Service Integrator Layer

Organizations who want to be a service integrator may already have ISO/IEC 20000 certification. Whilst this will give an independent assessment of the maturity and scope of their IT service management system and processes, it does not give any assessment of their capability in service integration.

ISO/IEC 20000 does not assess service integration processes, practices, policies or governance models. If a customer organization is using certification against ISO/IEC 20000 as one of the criteria for selecting an external service integrator, they will need to add specific service integration criteria.

Service integrators who want to be certified against ISO/IEC 20000 will find that many of the requirements of the standard do not fully align with the role of a service integrator.

For example, ISO/IEC 20000 does allow for external organizations to operate processes under the governance of the organization being certified. However, many Certification Bodies would find it a challenge to accept the situation where most process steps in the SIAM ecosystem are operated by external service providers, which will be the case for many SIAM implementations.

4.1.4.3. Service Provider Layer

A service provider that does not have ISO/IEC 20000 will be able to use the requirements of the standard as the basis for the development of the processes and policies that they require for SIAM.

However, they must compare these against the requirements from the service integrator. This might highlight potential conflicts between the requirements of ISO/IEC 20000 and the requirements of the SIAM model. It can sometimes be difficult for a service provider in a SIAM ecosystem to demonstrate that they have sufficient scope of control over their services, where the service integrator takes on some of these responsibilities.

For example, ISO/IEC 20000 expects a service provider to have contracts with other service providers that their services are dependent on. In a SIAM ecosystem, the customer will own the contracts with the service providers.

Service providers may already have certification against ISO/IEC 20000. This can be used as one of the criteria for selecting service providers for a SIAM ecosystem. Whilst this provides an independent assessment of the maturity and scope of their IT service management system and processes, it will not give any indication of their ability to operate in a SIAM ecosystem.

A service provider that already has ISO/IEC 20000 will need to compare how they have addressed the requirements from the standard with the requirements from the service integrator. Any changes necessary to comply with the SIAM ecosystem requirements need to be carefully considered in case they invalidate their ISO/IEC 20000 certification. The service provider may need to make a major change to the scope of their certification, and potentially be recertified.

4.2. Lean

4.2.1. What is Lean?

> The core idea of Lean is to maximize customer value while minimizing waste. Simply, lean means creating more value for customers with fewer resources.
>
> A lean organization understands customer value and focuses its key processes to continuously increase it. The ultimate goal is to provide perfect value to the customer through a perfect value creation process that has zero waste.[12]

Lean thinking started in the manufacturing sector as a way to:
- Improve efficiency
- Remove delays in delivery
- Reduce overall costs
- Improve quality.

Lean techniques focus on removing any activities or 'Muda' (waste) that don't add value to the finished product. This includes reviewing, and where appropriate removing:
- Double handling
- Wait times
- Unbalanced process flows
- Queues
- Constraints.

Lean thinking has since been applied to other sectors, including IT service management and IT. For example, Lean IT takes lean manufacturing principles and applies them to the development and management of IT products and services.

Agile is a development of Lean.

---

[12] Source: Lean Enterprise Institute

4.2.2. Lean in a SIAM Ecosystem

Using techniques from Lean can help to increase delivered value and maximise efficiencies in a SIAM model.

The techniques can deliver particular value when applied to processes. The application should start in the Plan and Build stage of the roadmap, to assist the design of efficient processes. Continual improvement should then be applied, using the same Lean thinking during the Implement and Run and Improve stages.

Every step in every process should be analyzed. Considerations should include:
- What value does this step add to the outputs from the previous step?
- Does that value contribute to the expected outputs from the whole process?
- Does this step repeat any work done in a previous step?
- Does this step repeat any work done in any other process?
- Are there any times during the step when no work is being carried out?
- Can the process step cope with the expected workload?

One of the key concepts from Lean is that quality should be designed into a product, not added into it by inspection. Wherever possible, processes should be designed to consistently deliver outputs with the required quality. Any subsequent quality inspections by the service integrator or customer should be examined to justify why they are required.

For example, consider the management of a change request sent from a service provider to the service integrator for approval, as shown in Table 1.

Process Step:	Potential Waste
Send change request to the service integrator	
Service integrator logs and reviews the change request	Pause in the process: the change request sits in an email inbox until read Double handling: change request has already been reviewed by the service provider
Service integrator's change manager assesses the change	Pause in the process: the change request sits in an email inbox until read Double handling: change request has already been assessed by the service provider
Change manager circulates the change request to the integrated change advisory board members	Pause in the process: the change manager only sends out change requests once a week
Integrated change advisory board members assess the change	Pause in the process: the change request sits in an email inbox until read No value added: Some board members don't have the skills or knowledge to assess the change
Integrated change advisory board schedule the change	Pause in the process: the board only meets once a week
Change manager authorizes deployment of the change	Pause in the process: the change manager doesn't authorize until the day after the Integrated change advisory board meeting

Table 1: management of a change request and sources of waste

4.3. COBIT®

4.3.1. What is COBIT®?

> COBIT® is a control framework for the governance and management of enterprise IT.[13]
>
> The latest version is COBIT 5®.

The official guide from ISACA documents the five principles of COBIT 5®:
1. Meeting stakeholder needs
2. Covering the enterprise end to end
3. Applying a single integrated framework
4. Enabling a holistic approach
5. Separating governance from management.

It also defines the seven supporting enablers that form the framework:
1. Principles, policies and frameworks
2. Processes
3. Organizational structures
4. Culture, ethics and behaviour
5. Information.
6. Services, infrastructure and applications
7. People, skills and competencies.

COBIT 5® includes:
- Framework to organise IT governance objectives and practices
  - Organizes IT governance objectives and good practices by IT domains and processes, and links them to business requirements
- Process descriptions
  - A reference process model and common language for everyone in an organization. The processes map to responsibility areas of plan, build, run and monitor

---

[13] Source: ISACA

- Control objectives
  - Provide a complete set of high-level requirements to be considered by management for effective control of each IT process
- Management guidelines
  - Help assign responsibility, agree on objectives, measure performance, and illustrate interrelationship with other processes
- Maturity models
  - Assess maturity and capability per process and helps to address gaps.

4.3.2. COBIT 5® in a SIAM Ecosystem

The five principles of COBIT® and the seven supporting enablers have clear synergies with SIAM as described in Section 2: SIAM Roadmap, Section 6: SIAM Practices, Section 7: SIAM Cultural Considerations, and the SIAM Foundation® Process Guide.

Table 2 shows how the COBIT® components can map to SIAM.

COBIT® Component	SIAM Component
Framework	Practices, governance model, structural elements
Process descriptions	Process models and processes
Control objectives	No direct equivalent
Management guidelines	Governance model
Maturity model	No direct equivalent

Table 2: COBIT® components and SIAM components

In a SIAM ecosystem, governance and management of information become more complex due to the number of stakeholders and organizations involved. The control objectives and maturity models from COBIT® can be particularly useful in addressing this complexity during the Discovery and Strategy and Plan and Build stages of the SIAM Roadmap.

Control objectives assist in defining the specific controls that should form part of the governance model. Maturity models help to define the current state during the discovery activities.

4.4. DevOps

4.4.1. What is DevOps?

> DevOps represents a change in IT culture, focusing on rapid IT service delivery through the adoption of agile, lean practices in the context of a system-oriented approach. DevOps emphasizes people (and culture), and seeks to improve collaboration between operations and development teams. DevOps implementations utilize technology — especially automation tools that can leverage an increasingly programmable and dynamic infrastructure from a life cycle perspective.[14]

DevOps embraces the full lifecycle of software development and operation. It is a flexible philosophy and approach, not a standard or a framework with prescriptive processes. DevOps thinking focuses on aspects including:

- Ownership and accountability
- Systems thinking
- Continual experimentation and learning
- Collaborative culture and sharing
- Automation
- Elimination of waste/Lean principles
- Measurement.

4.4.2. DevOps in a SIAM Ecosystem

4.4.2.1. Ownership and Accountability

DevOps is designed to deliver working software and solutions at pace, with a culture of full ownership and empowerment of the DevOps team.

---

[14] Source: Gartner

This can seem at odds with the governance and assurance roles of the service integrator, and it can cause tension with service providers who have adopted DevOps, as the service integrator can be considered to add delay to the implementation of change, with no added value.

DevOps uses the same team to specify, develop, test, deploy, and fully support services, including applications and infrastructure. This can conflict with the segregation of duties required in some SIAM models.

DevOps thinking can also conflict with SIAM sourcing approaches and grouping of services, where different service providers support infrastructure and applications. Most DevOps teams prefer to be responsible for all aspects of the service.

4.4.2.2. Culture and Sharing

The concepts from DevOps that relate to behaviour can be particularly useful in building a strong culture in SIAM ecosystems.

The focus on culture and sharing encourage collaboration and communication throughout the service lifecycle, using co-located multi-disciplinary teams who all share the goal of delivering outcomes that the customer wants.

For example, in a DevOps environment all members of the team are accountable for the success of a change; they take collective responsibility and accountability for approval. Contrast that with a typical IT service management approach that expects a single individual to be accountable. Using collective accountability for decisions in SIAM ecosystems can help to create the necessary collaborative culture.

4.4.2.3. Automation

Automation of activities such as testing and deployment is an important feature of DevOps.

Automation can speed up delivery and reduce risks. Automation needs to be integrated with the change management governance requirements in a SIAM ecosystem.

DevOps thinking can also help to address some common SIAM challenges, applying automation to overcome problems caused by a lack of integrated toolsets.

4.4.2.4. Continual Experimentation and Learning

An important DevOps concept is the incremental deployment of new functionality, followed by user feedback before the next increment.

This can be problematic in a SIAM ecosystem, as the deployment will impact multiple service providers.

If DevOps is adopted, the service providers and the service integrator will need to collaborate to build and maintain comprehensive automated test suites for the end to end services.

DevOps also encourages a culture of experimentation and learning in ways of working. Failures are a learning opportunity, not a blaming opportunity. This culture can be used to reinforce a culture of collaboration in a SIAM ecosystem.

4.5. Agile, Including Agile Service Management

4.5.1. What is Agile?

> Agile is a set of principles under which requirements and solutions evolve through the collaborative effort of self-organizing cross-functional teams.[15]

Agile thinking originated in software development. It used and built on Lean techniques from the manufacturing sector. In 2001, the Agile Manifesto was published which encapsulates the four values and twelve guiding principles for Agile.

---

[15] Source: Wikipedia

Agile thinking and the Manifesto have now been successfully applied in many different disciplines and situations, including project management, service management, DevOps, and SIAM.

Compared to traditional 'waterfall' approaches, Agile delivers changes more frequently, with smaller amounts of change delivered in each iteration. This provides a faster realization of benefits and reduced business risk.

The Agile approach also allows easier change of direction. For example, allowing a business to realize that a new service will not deliver the expected benefits before too much investment is made in its development.

Agile is a mind-set; it is not a set of processes. An organization doesn't 'do' Agile; it becomes Agile.

4.5.2. What is Agile Service Management?

> Agile Service Management (Agile SM) ensures that ITSM processes reflect Agile values and are designed with "just enough" control and structure in order to effectively and efficiently deliver services that facilitate customer outcomes when and how they are needed.[16]

The goals of Agile SM include:
- Ensuring that Agile values and principles are embedded into every service management process from design through implementation and continual improvement
- Improving IT's entire ability to meet customer requirements faster
- Being effective and efficient (Lean)
- Designing processes with "just enough" scalable control and structure
- Provide services that deliver ongoing customer value.

---

[16] Source: Agile Service Management Guide, © DevOps Institute 2015

4.5.3. Agile in a SIAM Ecosystem

Any SIAM implementation will benefit from a focus on the values of Agile.

The values from the Agile Manifesto can be adapted to apply in SIAM ecosystems; all parties in the ecosystem should value:
- Individuals and interactions over processes and tools
- Working services over comprehensive documentation
- Collaboration over contracts
- Responding to change over following a plan.

The items on the right have value, but priority should be given to the items on the left.

Agile approaches can be used to design, develop, and implement many parts of a SIAM model, SIAM structure, and a SIAM roadmap, including:
- Processes
- Policies
- Tooling
- Service improvements
- Structural elements.

Applying the four values and twelve guiding principles from the Agile Manifesto to IT service management and SIAM can:
- Improve delivery and the flow of work
- Improve customer satisfaction
- Support collaboration across the SIAM ecosystem
- Support incremental process improvement
- Provide flexibility
- Allow early identification of course corrections or changes of direction.

Table 3 provides some adapted examples of the twelve Agile principles, applied in a SIAM ecosystem.

Agile Principle	SIAM Application
The highest priority is to satisfy the customer through early and continuous delivery	Agile could be applied in a phased implementation of SIAM to address an issue with the current services, such as uncoordinated changes
Deliver releases frequently	The end to end change and release management processes and supporting governance should be designed to support rapid test, approval, and deployment of releases
Build projects around motivated individuals. Trust them to get the job done	The service integrator should trust the service providers and empower them to deliver their services without interference
Face to face conversation is the most efficient and effective method of conveying information	Working groups and process forums are an effective way to convey important information to service providers. Video conferencing and chat technology can be used to make this virtually 'face to face'
Continuous attention to excellence and good design enhances agility	Process forums can support the development and use of best practice across the service provider community
Simplicity is essential	The SIAM model should be understandable. If not, service providers may have difficulty in understanding and applying it
The best outputs emerge from self-organizing teams	Embodied in a SIAM environment through trust, empowerment, working groups and process forums
Reflect at regular intervals on how to become more effective, then tune and adjust behaviours	Process forums and governance boards should use data and information to identify areas for improvement, then action those improvements. Positive behaviours should be encouraged and rewarded

Table 3: examples of Agile principles applied in a SIAM ecosystem

4.5.4. Agile Service Management in a SIAM Ecosystem

Agile Service Management in a SIAM ecosystem can enable:

- Agile process design: uses agile techniques to design IT service management processes. These are designed and implemented in small, frequent releases; typically using 2 to 4 week cycles. The first cycle should deliver a Minimum Viable Process (MVP), which is the smallest amount of functionality that is needed. This enables early use and feedback, which is then fed into the next cycle
- Agile process improvement: uses agile techniques to improve processes. Within one service provider, the process owner should be empowered to improve their process. In the wider SIAM ecosystem, the process forum should be given that empowerment. Individual improvements should be designed and implemented using a regular, short cycle. The priority should be customer satisfaction. Lean thinking can be applied to find and remove waste and activities that add no value.

Summary
These, and other, practices can provide support to SIAM. Care should be taken to understand them in more detail, and to adapt them where required for use in a SIAM ecosystem.

5. SIAM Roles and Responsibilities

This section of the Body of Knowledge looks at roles and responsibilities in a typical SIAM ecosystem. This includes looking at the specific role of each SIAM layer, and the way that roles are grouped into structural elements.

A role is defined as *"the position or purpose that someone or something has in a situation, organization, society, or relationship"*[17]

A responsibility is defined as *"something that it is your job or duty to deal with"*[18]

5.1. Roles and the SIAM Roadmap

Within a SIAM ecosystem, roles and responsibilities need to be defined, allocated, monitored and improved.

Principles and policies for roles and responsibilities are defined during the Discovery and Strategy stage of the SIAM roadmap, before detail is added during Plan and Build. Roles and responsibilities are then allocated during the Implement stage and monitored during Run and Improve.

The four main activities related to roles and responsibilities are:

1. Definition of principles and policies
2. Design
3. Allocation
4. Monitoring and improvement.

5.1.1. Definition of Principles and Policies

Definition of the principles and policies for roles and responsibilities is a vital step in the design of the SIAM ecosystem.

---

[17] Source: Cambridge Dictionary
[18] Source: Cambridge Dictionary

During the Discovery and Strategy stage, existing roles and job descriptions are mapped and compared to required responsibilities (for instance, those defined within the governance framework) and the selected SIAM structure.

During the Discovery and Strategy stage, the roles and responsibilities themselves are not detailed; they are revisited and more detail is added during the design activities in the Plan and Build stage.

There is no single, ideal mapping of roles and responsibilities for a SIAM ecosystem. Each SIAM model will be different, depending on what the customer organization wishes to retain, and what it is prepared to source externally from the service integrator and/or the service providers.

The customer organization's decision about what to source internally, and what to source externally, will be influenced by several factors:

- The overall objectives for implementing SIAM
- The selected SIAM structure
- The customer's strategy and organizational goals
- Customer capability and skill levels
- What the customers regards as a strategic capability that is essential to retain
- Existing service provider relationships and outsourced roles and responsibilities.

The Service 'Menu'

We can think of this process as like choosing food from a menu. The customer is given the opportunity to review the roles and responsibilities and can select the options that are attractive to them.

This process puts the customer in control, allowing it to retain activities it sees as too risky or complex to outsource, and to transfer responsibility for tasks that it no longer wishes to undertake itself, or that can be effectively sourced externally.

5.1.2. Design
During the Plan and Build roadmap stage, detailed roles and responsibilities are designed using the outline SIAM model and outline process models, the SIAM structure and the governance framework.

5.1.3. Allocation
During the Implement stage, roles and responsibilities are allocated.

There are some roles that will always be allocated to specific SIAM layers:
- The customer organization must retain any roles that are mandated by legislation or regulations
- The service integrator will always be accountable for service governance, management, integration, assurance, and coordination, including end to end service management, service provider management, monitoring and reporting
- The service providers will fulfil service delivery roles.

5.1.4. Monitoring and Improvement
Once the roles and responsibilities are established, they are monitored to determine their effectiveness and to identify any opportunities for improvement. Improvements can be made to the individual roles and to the interfaces between roles.

Roles will need to be reviewed following any restructuring activities across the organization to ensure they remain aligned and effective.

5.2. How is a Role Different in a SIAM Ecosystem?
The definition of roles and responsibilities in a SIAM ecosystem must recognize that they will be applied in a multi-provider environment. Without careful design and management of roles and responsibilities, there is a higher risk that activities could be missed or duplicated as more parties are involved and the ecosystem is more complex.

> **Mapping Activities**
>
> In a SIAM ecosystem, one process or activity might span the three layers. For example, consider change management:
>
> - Customer layer: has input to change authorisation and scheduling
> - Service integrator layer: manages the integrated change management process
> - Service provider: initiates changes, presents them to the change advisory board, implements changes.
>
> There is also an opportunity for multiple roles to be performed by one person. For example, a process manager for a service provider might have:
>
> - A change management role, attending the change advisory board
> - A problem management role, attending a problem management working group
> - A knowledge management role, providing input into knowledge articles.
>
> The way that roles are allocated will depend on factors including the size and complexity of the SIAM ecosystem and resource availability and capability.

5.2.1. The Role of the Customer Organization

Outside of a SIAM model, it is usual for the customer to have a direct relationship with its service providers. In the SIAM ecosystem, the customer needs to understand that its role is to support and empower the service integrator. If the customer continues to work directly with service providers within a SIAM ecosystem, it may inadvertently create a 'Shadow IT' structure.

5.2.2. The Role of Retained Capabilities

For staff who are part of the retained capabilities, adapting to SIAM means relinquishing direct control of service providers and stepping back from day to day management of service provision. Their role needs to be strategic and proactive, rather than operational and reactive.

The retained capabilities role needs to have a strong relationship with the service integrator. Its purpose is to provide direction, and enable service integrator autonomy without creating a dictatorship.

The customer owns the contracts with the service providers, but the service integrator is managing delivery against them. The retained capabilities need to let the service integrator carry out its role without undermining it.

5.2.3. The Role of the Service Integrator

The role of the service integrator involves being the agent of the customer, acting on its behalf. This means doing the right thing for the customer, while not undermining its own organizational goals and objectives. The service integrator also represents the service providers and the end to end service to the customer organization.

The service integrator role relies on good relationships. To be effective, it must have a good relationship with the customer organization and the service providers.

The service integrator's role is to assure and facilitate service delivery. It needs to be contractually and commercially aware to carry out its role effectively in the SIAM ecosystem. The service integrator needs to focus on service integration and collaboration across multiple service providers.

5.2.4. The Role of Service Providers

Working collaboratively can be a new approach and a culture change for service providers. They need to adapt to working with potential competitors, and adjust to having a relationship with the service integrator rather than their customer.

They may have to change their ways of working and their structure to be effective in the SIAM ecosystem. Their role will require a focus on service objectives, balancing them against their own organizational objectives.

5.3. Role Description: Customer Organization, including Retained Capabilities

Description	The customer's role within the SIAM ecosystem is that of the commissioning organization. It also includes the retained capabilities that carry out corporate governance of the SIAM ecosystem.
Typical Accountabilities	<ul><li>Strategic direction</li><li>Enterprise architecture</li><li>Policy and standards management</li><li>Procurement</li><li>Contract management</li><li>Demand management</li><li>Financial and commercial management</li><li>Service portfolio management</li><li>Corporate risk management</li><li>Governance, including governance of the service integrator</li><li>Accountability for program and project management.</li></ul>
Typical Roles	<ul><li>Head of IT</li><li>Head of service</li><li>Service owner(s)</li><li>Enterprise architect</li><li>Service architect</li><li>Chief finance officer (CFO)</li><li>Chief information officer (CIO)</li><li>Chief security officer (CSO).</li></ul>
Typical Responsibilities	<ul><li>Defines and assures a core set of policies, standards, procedures and guidelines including architectural, informational, commercial, financial, security and enterprise service architecture</li><li>Develops and owns the IT strategy and strategy for SIAM that align with and support the business strategy</li><li>Develops and owns enterprise architecture, defines the technology, data and application roadmap, defines the service scope for SIAM</li><li>Provides overarching program and commercial management</li><li>Assures and governs the service integrator</li></ul>

	<ul><li>Manages the service provider relationships at an executive/commercial level</li><li>Overall management of risk</li><li>Resolves contractual disputes</li><li>Owns business relationships and acts as "intelligent customer" function</li><li>Defines end to end service budget.</li></ul>

5.4. Role Description: Service Integrator

Description	The service integrator layer of the SIAM model is where end to end service governance, integration, assurance and coordination are performed.
Typical Accountabilities	<ul><li>End to end service management</li><li>End to end performance management</li><li>End to end service reporting</li><li>Service governance and assurance</li><li>Tracking value for money</li><li>Continual service improvement.</li></ul>
Typical Roles	<ul><li>Head of service integration</li><li>Service delivery manager(s)</li><li>Service manager(s)</li><li>Process owner(s)</li><li>Process manager(s)</li><li>Service assurance manager(s)</li><li>Performance manager(s)</li><li>Security manager(s).</li></ul>
Typical Responsibilities	<ul><li>Responsible for end to end service management across the service providers and the interface into the customer organization</li><li>Managing service provider relationships at an operational level</li><li>Acting as the customer's "agent" and providing a communication path to the service providers</li><li>Managing end to end performance management of all service providers</li><li>Managing performance management of individual service providers against agreed targets</li><li>Coordination of the service providers</li><li>Assuring service provider performance and service delivery</li><li>Governing the service providers, as delegated by the customer organization</li><li>Facilitating process forums</li><li>Managing operational supply and demand for services and capacity</li><li>Consolidated service reporting</li><li>Providing service communications</li><li>Potential responsibility for provision and management of an integrated service management toolset</li><li>Managing the performance of service providers against contractual and service targets.</li></ul>

5.5. Role Description: Service Provider

Description	Within a SIAM ecosystem, there are multiple service providers. Each service provider is responsible for the delivery of one or more services, or service elements, to the customer. It is responsible for managing the products and technology used to deliver its contracted or agreed services. The service providers can be part of the customer organization or external to it.
Typical Accountabilities	<ul><li>Delivering services required by the customer to defined and agreed standards, policies and architecture</li><li>Exhibiting required behaviours for cooperation, collaboration, improvement and innovation</li><li>Ensuring cross-service provider service management processes are followed</li><li>Working collaboratively with suppliers and the service integrator to resolve issues, incidents and problems, identify improvement opportunities and meet customer outcomes.</li></ul>
Typical Roles	<ul><li>Service manager(s)</li><li>Account manager(s)</li><li>Process owner(s)</li><li>Process manager(s)</li><li>Technical staff</li><li>Service management staff.</li></ul>
Typical Responsibilities	<ul><li>Responsible for the delivery of technology and products to deliver services, at agreed service levels and cost</li><li>Integrating internal service management processes with the end to end service management processes</li><li>Adhering to policies, standards and procedures defined by the customer</li><li>Adhering to architectural design standards</li><li>Working collaboratively with the service integrator and other service providers</li><li>Taking part in structural elements, including process forums.</li></ul>

5.6. Governance Roles

Governance is a term that is widely used and often misunderstood. In a SIAM ecosystem, governance refers to the definition and application of policies and standards. These define and ensure the required levels of authority, decision making and accountability.

COBIT® 5 includes three activities in its definition of governance: evaluate, direct, and monitor. Lower level activities (plan, build etc.) are part of management.

This is shown in figure 14.

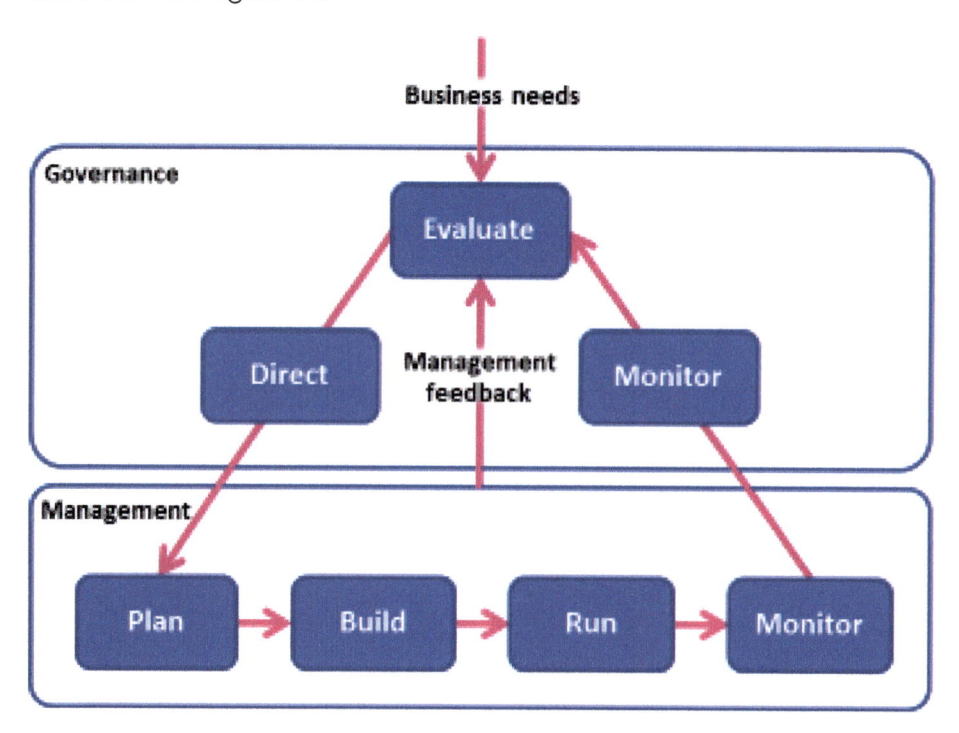

Figure 14 The COBIT 5 Business Framework for the Governance and Management of Enterprise IT ©, 2012, ISACA

The SIAM roles can be mapped onto this model, as shown in figure 15.

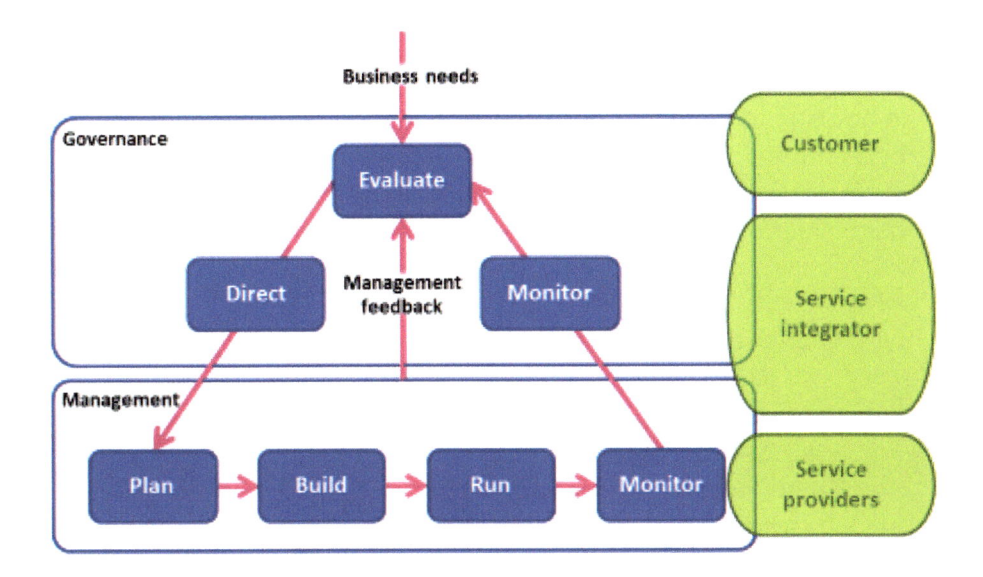

Figure 15 Mapping SIAM roles onto the COBIT 5 Business Framework

Governance activities are carried out at strategic, tactical and operational levels through governance boards. These boards form structural elements in the SIAM layers.

Boards are decision making bodies that are accountable for their decisions.
The boards discussed in this document provide the required level of governance in a SIAM environment. In complex environments with many different service providers, more boards might be created to address specific areas, for example:
- Information security advisory board
- IT service continuity governance board
- Program board.

The board structure that is put in place in a SIAM model needs to balance the level of overhead created by the board meetings against the governance requirements and the outcomes achieved.

5.6.1. Strategic Governance: Executive Boards

Executive boards provide governance and oversight at the most senior level. These boards also play an important role in establishing a SIAM culture, by demonstrating good behaviours at the most senior levels (see Section 7: SIAM Culture).

The attendees for these boards are senior staff with accountability for their organization's role in the SIAM model.
In addition to the executive board attended by all service providers, each service provider has an individual executive board with the customer and the service integrator. This allows a service provider to discuss commercial performance and sensitive issues.

5.6.1.1. Typical Attendees
Typical attendees include:
- Customer: chief information officer (CIO), chief technology officer (CTO), head of delivery or service delivery director
- Service integrator: operations director, contract and commercial director
- Service providers: operations director, contract and commercial director, account executive, CIO, CTO.

5.6.1.2. Typical Frequency
Executive boards are typically held quarterly.

5.6.1.3. Typical Agenda
An executive board agenda could include:
- Customer strategy: for the next six months, one year and three years
- Service integrator strategy updates, including any possible clashes or synergy, and opportunities for mutual benefit
- Service provider strategy updates, where appropriate, including any possible clashes or synergy, and opportunities for mutual benefit
- High-level review of last quarter, including successes and issues
- Contractual performance, including any obligations not being met; these are typically discussed at the individual

executive boards, unless there is a common issue across all service providers
- Planning for innovation, considering any new items from the service providers/service integrator
- Any other relevant topics.

5.6.1.4. Typical Inputs

Executive board inputs could include:
- Quarterly and monthly performance information
- Customer and service satisfaction information
- Customer strategy
- Strategic service improvements
- Strategic innovations
- Service integrator and service provider strategies, where relevant
- Service provider technology roadmap.

5.6.1.5. Typical Outputs

Executive board outputs could include:
- Action and decision logs
- Strategic course corrections or direction changes
- Business change requirements
- Strategic change schedule
- Celebration and communication of success.

5.6.2. Tactical Board

The tactical board sits between the strategic and operational boards. It forms part of the preparation for the operational board and can be used to carry out discussions before meeting with the customer, for example if a major incident has occurred. It can also be used to identify items for escalation to the strategic board, and acts as a point of escalation for operational boards.

This board is not attended by the customer.

5.6.2.1. Typical Attendees

Tactical board attendees are staff from the service integrator and the service providers. The roles present could include:
- Service delivery managers
- Service managers

- Process owners, as required
- Account managers.

5.6.2.2. Typical Frequency
Tactical boards are typically monthly.

5.6.2.3. Typical Agenda
This board is used to discuss service performance and continual improvement, so the agenda will vary depending on any issues that are being experienced.

The service integrator is empowered to interpret the contract on behalf of the customer so decisions might be made at this meeting about financial or non-financial remediation, which can then be communicated at the operational board.

This board will take direction from the strategic board and use it to create tactical action plans. It will also review changes escalated from the operational boards.

This board will include coordination, mediation, decision making, assurance and governance.

5.6.2.4. Typical Inputs
Tactical board inputs could include:
- Performance data, including customer satisfaction
- Service improvements
- Service provider data.

5.6.2.5. Typical Outputs
Tactical board outputs could include:
- Action and decision logs
- Tactical change schedule
- Improvement opportunities.

5.6.3. Operational Boards
The main operational board convenes to discuss service performance at a lower level than the executive and tactical boards.

It will review service performance and acts as an escalation point for all other operational boards and process forums. For example, it may authorize budget or resources to carry out improvement activities identified in a process forum that exceed the approval limit of the process forum attendees.

Other operational boards will be scheduled as required to support decision making; the most common example of this is the integrated change advisory board.

5.6.3.1. Typical Attendees
Operational board attendees could include:
- Customer retained capabilities, where required
- Service integrator
- Service providers
- User representatives
- Process owners
- Process managers
- Service managers.

5.6.3.2. Typical Frequency
Operational boards are typically monthly.

5.6.3.3. Typical Agenda
An operational board agenda could include:
- Review of monthly performance reports, including customer satisfaction
- Actions and decisions
- Critical and major incident reviews
- Escalations from other operational boards and process forums
- Six-monthly compliance and certification policies and procedures review.

5.6.3.4. Typical Inputs
Operational board inputs could include:
- Monthly reports
- Process reports; for example, incident reports
- Improvement plans
- Escalations from other operational boards

- Decisions from the tactical and strategic boards.

5.6.3.5. Typical Outputs

Operational board inputs could include:
- Decision and action logs
- Items for escalation
- Improvement actions.

5.6.4. Operational Board: Integrated Change Advisory Board

The integrated change advisory board is an operational governance board. It meets this definition because it makes decisions and is held accountable for them. It is chaired and managed by the service integrator.

This board reviews all changes within the scope of its authority that could affect the end to end service, regardless of which service provider will implement the change. It focuses on changes that affect multiple service providers, associated risks, and unintended impacts to the customer.

The board is also responsible for defining change policy. The policy defines the responsibilities for review and approval of different types of change. This includes the definition of standard or self-contained changes that can be approved locally by a service provider.

Where necessary, changes are escalated to the tactical or strategic boards. 'Review' of changes can encompass any action from detailed investigation through to definition of standard changes that gain automatic approval, or approval of systems for automated test and release (see Section 4.4: DevOps). The board seeks to facilitate, not prevent change.

The responsibilities of the integrated change advisory board include:
- Ensuring that all service providers and the customer are aware of relevant changes
- Confirming that:
    - Changes have been evaluated for risk and unintended impact
    - Remediation plans have been verified

- Appropriate resources have been allocated and made available to implement the change
- There are robust communication plans in place
- Ecosystem technical and architectural standards have been met
- Collective approval or otherwise of the change
- Creating mechanisms for standard changes and their automatic approval
- Review of completed changes.

5.6.4.1. Typical Attendees

Integrated change advisory board attendees could include:
- Service integrator change manager (chair)
- Service provider change managers
- Subject matter experts as required
- Customer representation as required.

5.6.4.2. Typical Frequency

The frequency of the integrated change advisory board varies, relating to the number and scale of changes. Additional emergency meetings can be convened as required.

5.6.4.3. Typical Agenda

An integrated change advisory board agenda could include:
- New changes to be reviewed
- Update on implemented changes and failed changes
- Improvements to the change management process.

5.6.4.4. Typical Inputs

Integrated change advisory board inputs could include:
- Change requests and related information
- Change management process performance information.

5.6.4.5. Typical Outputs

Integrated change advisory board outputs could include:
- Change status updates
- Process improvements.

5.7. Operational Roles

An effective SIAM ecosystem is built on working relationships and cultural alignment between all the SIAM layers.

At an operational level, working groups, boards and process forums all help to establish relationships and encourage communication between service providers and the service integrator. These working groups, boards and process forums form structural elements of the SIAM ecosystem, spanning the SIAM layers; see Section 1: Introduction to SIAM for more information.

There are many possible boards, process forums and working groups that can be implemented in a SIAM ecosystem, including:
- Integrated change advisory board
- Problem management forum
- Knowledge management forum
- Continual improvement forum
- Capacity management forum
- Information assurance and security forum
- Transition planning and support forum
- IT service continuity forum
- Service monitoring forum
- Incident management working group (for a specific incident or incidents)
- Release planning working group
- Problem management working group (for a specific problem or problems)
- Innovation working group (for a specific innovation).

The structural elements in place will vary in each SIAM ecosystem. A structural element can be created for any service management process or activity, if it supports improvements in service delivery and outcomes.

Forums can be combined where appropriate – for example, a single 'process improvement' forum could be used to assess possible improvements to multiple processes.

Combined forums are of value when processes have similar scope or have dependencies between their activities, for example change, configuration and release management. The number of meetings should always be balanced against the value of the meetings.

There are generic roles that will attend working groups and forums.

Process owner
- Accountable for end to end process design
- Accountable to process performance.

Both the service integrator and the service providers will have process owners. The service integrator process owner will be accountable for end to end process integration across the service providers.

The service provider process owner will be accountable for a process within the service provider and for alignment with the end to end process. A process owner is a role, so one staff member may act as the process owner for multiple processes.

Process manager
- Responsible for process execution.

In larger organizations, process manager roles are defined to support the process owner and be responsible for the execution of process activities.

Service owner
- Accountable to end to end service performance
- Defines service strategy
- Forecasts service demand and business requirements
- Service budget-holder.

This role will typically be part of the customer organization.

Service manager
- Responsible for service delivery for one or more services.

This role would typically be carried out by the service integrator.

Examples of Operational Roles

This section provides some examples of process forums and working groups in a SIAM ecosystem. These examples can be used as the basis for the design of other process forums and working groups within a SIAM model.

5.7.1. Knowledge Management Forum

The Knowledge Management Forum is hosted and managed by the service integrator knowledge management process owner.

It is a regular forum where the performance and effectiveness of knowledge management across the ecosystem is reviewed and assessed.

5.7.1.1. Typical Attendees

Knowledge management forum attendees could include:
- Service integrator knowledge management process owner (chair)
- Service provider knowledge management process owners/process managers
- Service integrator service manager as required
- Subject matter experts as required
- Customer representation as required.

5.7.1.2. Typical Frequency

Process forums are typically monthly.

5.7.1.3. Typical Responsibilities

Knowledge management forum responsibilities could include:
- Reviewing accuracy and currency of the knowledge articles in use
- Identifying new knowledge articles that are required based on repeat incidents or requests received by the service desk
- Allowing service providers to collaborate on identifying any incident types that could be resolved at the service desk or via self-help systems rather than by second line teams, improving the end user experience.

5.7.2. Continual Improvement Forum

The continual improvement forum is hosted and managed by the service integrator.

It is a cross-ecosystem forum attended by all service providers and the customer. Attendees can present, discuss and agree initiatives for improvement; for example, ways to deliver cost savings or improve customer experience.

5.7.2.1. Typical Attendees
Continual improvement forum attendees could include:
- Service integrator continual improvement process owner (chair)
- Service provider continual improvement process owners/process managers
- Service integrator delivery manager/director
- Service owners
- Other process owners as required
- Subject matter experts as required
- Customer representation as required.

5.7.2.2. Typical Frequency
Process forums are typically monthly.

5.7.2.3. Typical Responsibilities
Continual improvement forum responsibilities could include:
- Presenting and reviewing ideas for improvement
- Assessing the potential of initiatives
- Prioritization of initiatives
- Agreeing the responsible party or parties to implement the improvement; this may involve cross-service provider collaboration and implementation
- Approval of any budgetary spend (this may need to be escalated to a governance board)
- Communicating the benefits to the business
- Tracking the progress and ultimate success of the improvements.

5.7.3. Major Incident Working Group

The major incident working group is chaired and managed by the service integrator. It may also be referred to as a crisis team, critical incident team or major incident bridge.

It is convened during a major incident, to coordinate the response, facilitate cross-service provider communication and provide regular updates to the customer organization.

Any lessons learned during a major incident will be discussed in the incident management process forum.

5.7.3.1. Typical Attendees
Major incident working group attendees could include:
- Service integrator major incident manager (chair)
- Service provider incident management process owners/process managers
- Other process owners as required
- Subject matter and technical experts as required
- Service owners as required
- Customer representation as required.

5.7.3.2. Typical Frequency
A major incident working group will be held when required; when a major incident has occurred.

5.7.3.3. Typical Responsibilities
Major incident working group responsibilities could include:
- Coordinating major incident investigation and resolution
- Coordinating major incident communications
- Encouraging a 'fix first, argue later' culture.

5.8. The Service Desk in a SIAM Ecosystem

The role of the service desk and how it is sourced will vary from SIAM ecosystem to ecosystem.

The service desk is often seen as a good candidate for external sourcing due to high staff turnover and management overhead, but some companies prefer to keep it internal or use a hybrid approach.

The organization providing the service desk will be treated and managed as a service provider in the SIAM ecosystem, whether it is provided by the customer organization, the service integrator or a service provider.

Within a SIAM ecosystem, the service desk acts as a 'single source of truth' and provides important management information about service performance. If the service integrator is not providing the service desk, it must work very closely with it and use the service data it provides.

Some of the potential sourcing options are:
1. The customer organization provides the service desk and associated toolset, acting as an internal service provider, and routes incidents to service providers as necessary
2. The service integrator provides the service desk and associated toolset
3. An external service provider provides the service desk and toolset, but no other services
4. An external service provider provides the service desk and toolset in addition to other services; this is often combined with end user computing, applications or hosting
5. Different service providers provide their own service desks and toolsets and the service integrator provides a consolidated view; this is only possible where it is clear to the customer which service desk to contact for support.

In most instances, the end user contacts a single service desk, which then works with the relevant service provider service desks and support teams. The end user has a single point of contact.

The staff who work on the service desk will require similar skills to those outside of a SIAM ecosystem, but they will also need:
- Supplier management skills
- Commercial awareness.

These skills will allow them to work successfully with different service providers, who may have different contracts, service targets and responsibilities.

6. SIAM Practices

Practices are defined as: *the actual application or use of an idea, belief, or method, as opposed to theories relating to it.*[19]

From a SIAM perspective, 'practices' meet this definition when organizations are applying them within a SIAM model. The examples in this section give some illustrations of how to apply SIAM in the real world.

Within SIAM there are four types of practice:
1. People practices
2. Process practices
3. Measurement practices
4. Technology practices.

This section of the Body of Knowledge looks at one area for each practice type. It considers the challenges associated with that area, and then the working practices that can be used to address the challenges.

These example practices should not be thought of as 'good' or 'best' practice. They provide an illustration of how practices can work in a SIAM ecosystem.

SIAM also draws on practices from other areas of IT and management; see Section 4: SIAM and Other Practices.

6.1. People Practices: Managing Cross-functional Teams

"A cross-functional team is a group of people with different functional expertise working toward a common goal. It may include people from finance, marketing, operations, and human

---

[19] Source: Oxford English Dictionary © 2016 Oxford University Press

resources departments. Typically, it includes employees from all levels of an organization."[20]

The SIAM Ecosystem and Cross-functional Teams
With the SIAM ecosystem, cross-functional teams will have members from different organizations and different SIAM layers. These teams are referred to as "structural elements"

There are three types of structural element/cross-functional team:
1. Boards
2. Process forums
3. Working Groups.

These are described in Section 1: Introduction to SIAM and Section 5: Roles and Responsibilities.

> In a SIAM environment, examples of cross-functional teams could include:
>
> **A major incident working group** where the cause is unclear. The team includes staff from the service integrator and multiple service provider organizations. Team members need to work together towards a shared outcome (incident resolution), whilst meeting service requirements and balancing their own organizational goals.
>
> **The integrated change advisory board** involving staff from the customer organization, service integrator and multiple service providers. The team members work together to review, prioritise, risk assess and approve or reject changes to an integrated service.

6.1.1. Challenges Related to Cross-functional Teams
Some of the main challenges associated with cross-functional teams are:
1. Conflicting objectives, organizational strategies and working practices
2. Reluctance to share knowledge
3. Lack of automation.

---

[20] Source: Wikipedia

6.1.1.1. Conflicting Objectives, Organizational Strategies and Working Practices

The cross-functional teams in a SIAM ecosystem contain staff from multiple service providers, the service integrator and, in some cases, from the customer organization as well. This can create challenges when staff must balance their own organizational objectives with cross-functional team objectives.

For example, during a major incident, a service provider's organizational goals might be to demonstrate that it is not responsible for causing the incident, and to minimize the resources allocated to resolving it.

However, the end to end service targets could be focused on resolving the incident and then assessing what caused it later. This requires the service provider to adopt a 'fix first, argue later' approach which may conflict with its individual organizational goals.

Differences between organizational strategies and working practices can also have an impact on the performance of a cross-functional team.

For example, technical organizations might prioritize resolving incidents above customer communication. In a SIAM ecosystem, they might have to prioritize customer communication over service restoration.

6.1.1.2. Reluctance to Share

The service provider and service integrator staff working in a SIAM ecosystem need to share information, and collaborate at a people, process and technology level.

In an effective SIAM ecosystem, they may have targets relating to service improvement as well as service delivery.
To innovate effectively and improve service delivery, service providers and the service integrator need to work together. Some organizations may be reluctant to do this because they view it as sharing their intellectual property with a competitor.

6.1.1.3. Lack of Automation

Lack of automation and ineffective toolsets can also be a challenge for cross-functional teams. Where more than one toolset is in use, poor integration between tools is also a challenge.

The issues here can include:
- Inability to measure end to end team performance
- Inability to easily share information between teams
- Duplicated work caused by entering data into multiple toolsets (the 'swivel chair' approach)
- Reduced likelihood of identifying patterns or opportunities for improvement
- Reduced workflow automation, leading to workflow interruptions, delays, and an inability to monitor workflow.

6.1.2. Practices for Managing Cross-functional Teams

To support effective management of cross-functional teams, the service integrator and the customer need to consider:
1. Roles and responsibilities
2. Clear goals and objectives
3. Knowledge, data and information
4. Communication
5. Toolset integration.

6.1.2.1. Roles and Responsibilities

Defining clear principles and policies for roles and responsibilities as part of the Discovery and Strategy stage of the SIAM roadmap will lay the foundation for better cross-functional working.

This supports communication within cross-functional teams because all the parties involved have a clear understanding of who the stakeholders are.

RACI matrices are a useful tool for mapping roles and responsibilities in cross-functional teams.

RACI Matrix

RACI matrices are used to manage resources and roles for the delivery of an activity or task. They can be used to identify all participants in the delivery of a process or function.

Resources can be drawn from different functional areas and organizations, so a RACI matrix is used to track who is doing what, identifying interfaces and engagement with other roles. It provides a clear mapping of roles across the different teams in the SIAM ecosystem.

RACI stands for Responsible, Accountable, Consulted and Informed.

Only one role can be **Accountable** for a task. The role that is accountable for the task has the overall authority - but might not carry out individual pieces of work him/herself.

Any number of roles can be **Responsible** as part of the RACI model. These are the workers who will get the actual tasks done, and they will report to the Accountable resource about their progress.

Sometimes roles are **Consulted** to get a task done. This might be a person within the organization who has specific knowledge, or it could be a document store or even an internet search engine. These resources need to be tracked to ensure they are available when required.

Other roles need to be **Informed**. These resources are stakeholders who need to track and understand exactly how the task is proceeding, or they may need an output from the activity. Customer organization sponsors, for example, will typically be informed about progress as part of a project.

To build a RACI matrix, these steps need to be followed:
- Identify activities
- Identify roles
- Assign RACI codes
- Identify gaps or overlaps that need resolving
- Distribute the chart for feedback

- Deploy to all relevant parties
- Monitor the roles
- Apply improvements or changes based on feedback and experience.

6.1.2.2. Clear Goals and Objectives

As well as a clear understanding of roles and responsibilities, parties in a SIAM ecosystem need clear goals and objectives.

- The customer will define the strategic objectives for the services
- The objectives will be translated into contracts and service agreements
- The service integrator will work with service providers to:
    - Develop process goals and objectives that drive process execution
    - Develop operational level agreements or targets that align with the contracts and service agreements.

Whilst it is important that each service provider has measurable service targets to work towards, they need to be part of an end to end performance management and reporting framework. This will, in turn, provide evidence of demonstrable achievement of service objectives, business benefits or value.

If there is no clear definition and communication of value, or end to end metrics, service providers may focus only on their own performance and not see the end to end view.

In some cases, it might be acceptable for a service provider to miss a target in one area, because it means meeting a target in a different area. The service integrator can help the service providers to prioritize when there is a conflict between individual targets and end to end service targets.

6.1.2.3. Knowledge, Data and Information

Cross-functional teams need access to shared knowledge, data and information.

When these are not shared or readily available:
- Team members will waste time re-discovering or recreating them
- Service issues and customer contacts might be managed in inconsistent ways
- Work will not be carried out in the most efficient way
- Different parties may have different 'versions of the truth'.

The service integrator needs to create a knowledge management strategy and policy to govern how knowledge is gathered, processed, presented, managed and removed.

The service integrator will also make sure that all service providers have access to the knowledge they need as part of a shared knowledge repository. All service providers should contribute to this repository for the benefit of all other parties.

Checks need to be in place to make sure knowledge is updated, relevant, and being used.

6.1.2.4. Communication

The service integrator and the service providers need to communicate regularly and work to build relationships and trust. The RACI matrix developed as part of the roles and responsibilities definition is useful to define the 'who', 'what', 'when', 'where', 'how' and 'why' of communication.

A communication plan is key to ensure that:
- All stakeholders and their communication requirements are identified
- There is an appropriate level of regular communication for all stakeholders, for example meetings and levels of reporting
- Communication takes place at the right level for each layer of the SIAM ecosystem
- Communication is consistent across service providers

- Effective communication channels are selected to support timeliness, relationship building, ease of execution and access.

Use of the various structural elements in the SIAM ecosystem (including boards, process forums, and working groups) will help to build relationships and encourage better cross-functional working.

Virtual Teams

In a SIAM ecosystem, team members are likely to be in different geographical locations. These are referred to as 'virtual teams'.

The resources in the teams might also have multiple customers to work with; for example, a service provider's technical support staff might be involved in more than one SIAM engagement.

The service integrator needs to carefully consider how to manage communication within these teams. Even more care is required if teams are virtual as well as cross-functional.

Virtual teams need to build relationships between team members. This can be challenging if there is no regular face to face contact between them. It is recommended to have at least one face to face event where team members can get to know each other, to foster trust and create good working relationships.

Tools can be used to support communication in virtual teams. Examples are videoconferencing, social media, and chat tools.

6.1.2.5. Toolset Integration

For cross-functional teams, integration between toolsets will save time and resources, and reduce the possibility of errors. It can also support workflow automation.

Integrating toolsets will reduce the need to re-enter and translate data. There is less chance of information errors leading to friction between teams.

6.2. Process Practices: Integrating Processes across Service Providers

Within the context of this document, a process is *"a documented, repeatable approach to carrying out a series of tasks or activities"*.

SIAM Environments and Integrated Processes

> In a SIAM environment, processes must operate effectively and efficiently across multiple parties. This includes service providers, the service integrator, and sometimes, the customer.
>
> For example, during change management, the service integrator is accountable for changes to integrated services, across all the service providers involved with the change.
>
> Change management includes change recording, assessment, prioritization, planning, approval, and post-implementation reviews.
>
> The service providers, the service integrator, and potentially the customer will all be involved. This requires a change management process that is integrated across all parties.

6.2.1. Challenges Related to Integrating Processes across Service Providers

Challenges associated with integrating processes across service providers include:
1. Service providers do not integrate their processes or share process details
2. Gaps between process activities
3. Time-consuming and manual reporting
4. Poor relationships between service providers/blame culture.

6.2.1.1. Service Providers do not Integrate their Processes or Share Process Details

Within a SIAM ecosystem, data and information must flow between all parties. This does not mean that all parties must use the same process. Instead, each service provider and the service integrator must work together to ensure their processes are aligned to deliver the required outcome.

This requires processes from the service providers, the service integrator, and the customer to be aligned and integrated. Some of the service providers in a SIAM ecosystem may be unwilling, or unable, to make the adaptations necessary to support this integration.

This may be acceptable if outcomes and performance meet the pre-defined targets. However, unless this is considered in the design of the integrated processes it can result in:
- Adversely affected outcomes
- Failure to meet end to end service levels
- Inefficiencies in the execution of the integrated processes
- Unforeseen additional overheads in the service integrator
- Miscommunication.

For example, consider a situation where one of the services is a cloud based commodity email service.

The service provider will publish planned changes and service outages on its website. It will not directly inform the service integrator, seek approval for changes, or attend any change management boards. The service integrator must regularly check the service provider's website. The service integrator informs the other service providers and customer of any changes that will affect them.

6.2.1.2. Gaps Between Process Activities

Process integration fails when there is a gap or a break in the process flow.

This could be a simple action; for example, an incident being assigned to a queue for a service provider, and not being picked up, resulting in increased downtime for the customer. Gaps are often identified when process performance targets are failed, for example, when incident resolution times are missed.

These gaps need to be identified and addressed during Plan and Build and on an ongoing basis. The development and agreement of process flows and RACI matrices (see Section 6.1.2) will help to identify and avoid such gaps.

Gaps should also be identified during the service integrator assurance activities.

6.2.1.3. Time-consuming and Manual Reporting

Where different providers use different processes, it is likely that they will also use different toolsets. The use of different toolsets can affect the ability, effectiveness, and efficiency of the monitoring and reporting on performance of end to end processes.

Unless this is recognized and managed during the Plan and Build stage, monitoring and reporting for end to end processes can be time consuming and laborious. Design activities must recognize this, to ensure that the value of the information produced justifies the effort required to collect and process it.

6.2.1.4. Poor Relationships between Service Providers/Blame Culture

The success of an integrated process depends on all parties contributing to its design, execution, and improvement. Service providers are less likely to contribute if their relationships with other service providers and with the service integrator are poor.

Service providers need to adopt a 'fix first, argue later' mentality to resolve issues. This needs to be supported by a 'no blame' culture so that service providers are ready to be open about their faults rather than trying to hide them.

The 'no blame' culture needs to start with the customer and then be continually reinforced by the service integrator to create a collaborative environment. This will assist with building the necessary good relationships.

6.2.2. Practices for Integrating Processes across Service Providers

Practices for integrating processes across service providers include:
1. Focus on process outcomes
2. Continual process improvement
3. Establishing process forums.

In addition to these practices, the RACI matrices mentioned in Section 6.1.2 will also be helpful for identifying the role and responsibility of each stakeholder for each process activity.

6.2.2.1. Focus on Process Outcomes

The service integrator needs to be clear about the outcome that a process is expected to deliver. This can then be communicated to the service providers so that they all understand their role and responsibilities within the process.

It is better to start with the outcome and then work back, rather than to start with lower level steps and activities in the hope that they can be brought together into a process. For each process that involves multiple parties, these items should be documented and understood:

- Inputs
- Outputs
- Outcomes
- Interactions
- Dependencies
- Controls
- Data and information standards
- Process steps
- Process flow.

RACI matrices can help to document these, and are a commonly used and widely understood technique.

It is important to recognize and reward positive outcomes when processes are performing well.

6.2.2.2. Continual Process Improvement

All processes should be subject to review and improvement measures. This continual improvement can be managed on multiple levels:

- Within each area responsible for the provision and fulfilment of the process
- At the process level, for example via the process forums or the process owner.

These levels should also feed into an overall process improvement program run by the service integrator. This is particularly relevant when an improvement is dependent on resources external to the process or is likely to have a significantly beneficial impact.

Each process will have a process owner who will be accountable for continual improvement across the end to end process, and the service integrator has ultimate accountability for process improvement.

Process improvements should be assessed, justified and approved using an agreed mechanism, often in the process forum. Once improvements are implemented their benefits should be tracked to confirm an improvement has been delivered. This can be more challenging in a SIAM ecosystem than for a process that exists within a single organization.

6.2.2.3. Establishing Process Forums

Process forums are a type of structural element within a SIAM model. They are used to bring together process owners from the service providers and the service integrator. Their purpose is to work together on the design and improvement of how their process supports end to end delivery.

This includes:
- Defining data and information standards
- Identifying and managing process improvements
- Developing and sharing good practice
- Sharing information
- Assessing and improving capability and maturity.

Process forums are invaluable for building relationships and trust between all parties. They can be established for any process in the SIAM ecosystem.

6.3. Measurement Practices: Enable and Report on End to End Services

End to end service measurement refers to the ability to monitor an actual service, not just its individual technical components or providers.

Effective measurement practices support the performance management and reporting framework.

SIAM Environments and End to End Service Measurement

> In a SIAM environment, examples of end to end measurement could include:
>
> **The percentage of service downtime related to failed changes:** based on the number of changes implemented and the number that failed, where the impact of failure was felt by the customer
>
> **Responsiveness of the service against defined targets:** based on measuring the customer's actual experience of the service, not just individual elements, such as network speed or application responsiveness
>
> End to end measurement is more complex in a SIAM environment because more than one service provider is involved with service delivery. The end to end view is aggregated by the service integrator using data from all service providers.

6.3.1. Challenges Related to Enabling and Reporting on End to End Services

Challenges associated with measurement of end to end services include:
1. Lack of strategic requirements
2. Reluctance to share information
3. Inability to map end to end service architecture
4. Not measuring the correct amount of data and information.

6.3.1.1. Lack of Strategic Requirements

An effective performance management and reporting framework can only be built once it is clear what needs to be measured.

If the overall strategic requirements for the services are unknown, it will be difficult to create a meaningful set of end to end measurements and reports.

6.3.1.2. Reluctance to Share Information

Poor relationships or competitive tension between service providers can lead to an unwillingness to share information. Service providers might also be reluctant to share information if they feel it will be used to punish them, rather than as a source of learning and improvement.

In some situations, the customer withholds information from the service integrator. If the service integrator is an external organization, for example, the customer might not want to share some information that it considers to be confidential.

6.3.1.3. Inability to Map End to End Service Architecture

Many organizations struggle to map an end to end service, and understand what is in scope for measurement and what is not. With the addition of multiple service providers and a distributed architecture, this can be even more challenging.

The service integrator needs to map the end to end service and work with each service provider to confirm what needs to be measured to build the end to end picture. Enabling practices like OBASHI and configuration management can be of assistance in this.

6.3.1.4. Not Measuring the Correct Amount of Data and Information

Some organizations do not collect enough data, and some collect too much.

If an organization does not collect enough, there is a risk that important information will be missed. If they collect too much, there is a risk that there is too much data to analyze, which can also lead to important information being missed.

The same is true for how much information is included in reports. Small amounts of information may seem easier to understand but may hide important information. Large amounts may be difficult to understand and can complicate the ability to present an accurate picture.

The challenge is to identify the optimum amount of information to collect and report on. A useful technique is to report at a summary level but have the detailed reports available to support any requirement for more in-depth information.

6.3.2. Practices for Enabling and Reporting on End to End Services

Practices for enabling and reporting on end to end services include:
1. Create a performance management and reporting framework
2. Make reports visual
3. Use qualitative and quantitative measures
4. Apply agile thinking.

6.3.2.1.   Create a Performance Management and Reporting Framework

A performance management and reporting framework provides a way to structure data and information from service measurement and link them to the customer organization's strategic requirements.

The performance management and reporting framework will be created during the Plan and Build roadmap stage.

Performance management and reporting frameworks can be structured in a variety of ways, depending on the available toolset, the strategic requirements and the service contracts.

Possible framework structures include:
1. By SIAM ecosystem layers:
   - Service provider metrics
   - Service integrator metrics
   - Customer metrics.

2. By type:
   - People metrics
   - Process metrics
   - Technology metrics.

3. By hierarchy, allowing for information to be expanded or shown in more detail when needed:
   - Strategic metrics
   - Tactical metrics
   - Operational metrics.

6.3.2.2. Make Reports Visual

Information is most effective when it is visual and easy to understand. Using service dashboards and scorecards will increase the impact of reporting.

A picture can be easier to understand than a long report, but care must be taken to clearly identify each visual and what it indicates.

6.3.2.3. Use Qualitative and Quantitative Measures

Quantitative measures are numerical, and factual; for example, the number of incidents that were resolved in the agreed timescales, or a reduction in the number of target breaches.

Qualitative measures are usually descriptive and often in non-numerical form; for example, customer satisfaction surveys.

Whilst it is relatively easy to measure and report on quantitative measures, they do not often reflect the quality of the service accurately. One of the drivers for SIAM is the 'watermelon' effect, where service providers report they are meeting all their targets, but the customer is still not happy. Using a mix of qualitative and quantitative measures will help to provide a balanced view. Care should be taken to ensure that these remain aligned to strategic requirements and service objectives.

The Watermelon Effect

The watermelon effect occurs when a report is 'green on the outside, red on the inside'.

The service provider(s) meet individual targets, but the end to end service is not meeting the customer's requirements. This does not deliver a good outcome for the customer, and should also be a concern for the service provider.

It may be good for the service provider to be meeting its targets, but if their customer is not happy they will not have a good long term relationship.

In this situation, the target is not aligned to business requirements.

6.3.2.4. Apply Agile Thinking

The application of Agile techniques can help to determine the optimum amount of information in reports. Start by reporting on a minimum set of viable metrics. These can provide the minimum amount of information to assess performance, with no unnecessary additions or duplication.

These reports can then be used as the basis for discussion and learning, with more measurements being added if required.

It is often beneficial to start small and then develop the performance management and reporting framework. This approach should initially use less resource than trying to measure every single element of the ecosystem.

See Section 4: SIAM and Other Practices for more information about SIAM and Agile.

6.4. Technology Practices: Creating a Tooling Strategy

A tooling strategy outlines the requirements for a toolset or toolsets to support the SIAM ecosystem. It will include functional and non-functional requirements, the processes that need to be supported, standards for interfacing to the toolset(s) and a roadmap for future development.

Typically, organizations will focus on the IT service management tool, which will support processes including incident, problem, change, configuration, release management and request fulfilment. However, there are other areas where a tooling strategy will provide considerable benefit, such as:

- Event management
- Event correlation
- Software asset management
- Discovery
- Capacity, performance and availability management
- Operational risk management
- Project management
- Service performance reporting.

SIAM Environments and the Tooling Strategy

> An optimized tooling strategy will make it easier for the service providers in a SIAM ecosystem to work together. It can also:
> - Help the service integrator to get a 'real time' view of end to end service performance
> - Improve the efficiency of workflow
> - Support data integration, which is critical in establishing aggregated service views from data provided by multiple service providers
>
> There are several possible approaches for tooling. These are listed in Section 2: the SIAM Roadmap. The aim is to have integration between all toolsets.
>
> Integration is difficult to achieve, relying on sophisticated data mapping between service providers and the service integrator. Toolset integration requirements need to be documented and assessed in the context of the broader technology architecture.
>
> In some circumstances, it may be acceptable to use less sophisticated and more manual methods (often referred to as 'loose coupling' of data exchange). For time-critical activities like major incident management, there may be little alternative other than to build integration between toolsets (referred to as 'tight coupling' of data exchange).
>
> The integrated toolset acts as a single version of the truth for all the parties in the SIAM ecosystem, simplifying data transfer, reporting and accuracy.

6.4.1. Challenges Related to Creating a Tooling Strategy

Challenges associated with creating a tooling strategy include:
1. Ineffective legacy tools
2. Defining the toolset scope
3. Non-compliant service providers
4. Lack of architecture.

6.4.1.1. Ineffective Legacy Tools

The customer organization may require the service integrator and/or service providers to use legacy toolsets that it already has in place. This can lead to several challenges:

- The toolset may not support all the processes in the SIAM ecosystem
- It may not support the use of integrated processes
- It will contain legacy data which may be challenging to adapt to the new environment
- It may be difficult to interface with the service providers and service integrators toolsets
- If the service integrator is external, they may not have any expertise in the toolset.

6.4.1.2. Defining the Toolset Scope

A SIAM ecosystem can include many processes, some of which are outside the 'standard' set of IT service management processes.

The tooling strategy should encompass all the processes in the SIAM model, and recognize that the ideal solution may be a hybrid of various tools, to support the functional requirements of each process and the broader SIAM ecosystem.

The toolset also needs to support end to end process control, not just operational execution. More tool vendors are now creating functionality that supports a SIAM ecosystem.

6.4.1.3. Non-compliant Service Providers

If the tooling strategy requires that all parties use the same toolsets, some potential service providers may be unwilling to be part of the SIAM ecosystem.

If the tooling strategy is that service providers integrate their own tools with the service integrators toolset, some may be unwilling or unable to configure the integration. For example, providers of commodity cloud services may have little flexibility in their offerings.

The tooling strategy needs careful consideration at the Discovery and Strategy and Plan and Build stages of the SIAM Roadmap, as it has influence on and dependencies within the SIAM structures and the overall SIAM model. The strategy must also consider the data and information standards.

Once they have been agreed, requirements from the tooling strategy should be included in any contracts with service providers and any external service integrator. This is because a non-compliant service provider can lead to inefficiencies in cross-provider processes, reporting, and gaps between service providers.

6.4.1.4. Lack of Architecture

The absence of an enterprise architecture and technical architecture for the SIAM ecosystem and services will create challenges related to the selection of toolsets, and the definition of interfaces between toolsets.

The architecture documents need to address:
- The need for data sovereignty/visibility requirements to be addressed through role based access controls. For example, service providers may not be able to be view each other's targets or performance
- The need for robust data integration capabilities. Some organizations choose to build an 'enterprise service bus' or messaging engine into their technology architectures to cater for this requirement
- The need for all data update activities to be auditable and traceable
- The need for all parties in the SIAM eco-system to be familiar with the tooling strategy and the specific tools to be deployed, not only so they can develop any integrations as necessary, but also to ensure that their staff are adequately trained in their use.

The toolset architecture must support the tooling strategy.
The service providers of the toolsets themselves must be treated as a service provider within the SIAM ecosystem, because the effective operation of the SIAM model is dependent on their services.

6.4.2. Practices Related to Creating a Tooling Strategy
Practices associated with creating a tooling strategy include:
1. Technology strategy and roadmap
2. Industry standard integration methods
3. Ownership of data and toolsets
4. Ease of adding and removing service providers
5. Adopting a common data dictionary.

6.4.2.1. Technology Strategy and Roadmap
The customer organization needs to outline its technology strategy and roadmap, to help the service integrator and the service providers understand how the SIAM toolset will integrate and evolve.

The customer also needs to share any functional and technical requirements, for example if the toolset must meet certain security specifications.

6.4.2.2. Industry Standard Integration Methods
Using industry standard integration methods will make it easier for service providers to share information between their own tools and an integrated SIAM toolset. This will make it easier to create interfaces, and should reduce the need for expensive development and customization.

The integration approach adopted should not just cater for data transmission, but also for error handling in the event of issues occurring.

Given the potential criticality of the integration, consideration should also be given to service continuity requirements. Both the production and any back up or continuity environments should be tested to ensure that they meet the functional and non-functional requirements required by the customer.

6.4.2.3. Ownership of Data and Toolsets
When the service integrator role is being taken by an external organization, the tooling strategy needs to clarify who owns the toolset, and the data within it.
If the external service integrator owns the toolset (for example), the customer needs to ensure it still has data access if the commercial relationship ends; or define how the data will be migrated at such time.

In addition, the toolset must be placed under change control, particularly if data integration exists. If changes are made by any party to their toolsets, this can have unexpected effects on the integrity of the supporting data integrations described above, if data fields or values change.

6.4.2.4. Ease of Adding and Removing Service Providers

One of the benefits of a SIAM ecosystem is the ability to add and remove service providers easily.

The tooling strategy needs to support this. When a new service provider is added, it needs to be easy for that organization to adopt the toolset, including set-up of local toolset interfaces and training its staff.

When a service provider is removed, it must be simple to remove its access to the toolset and ensure that data is stored or (re)moved as required.

6.4.2.5. Adopting a Common Data Dictionary

The toolset should be used to enforce a common data dictionary. This will deliver several benefits, for example giving consistency and a common understanding of incident priority and severity classifications.

There will be confusion if one service provider's 'priority 1' incident is another service provider's 'severity 3'. This activity should be undertaken for all data fields in the toolset.

The data dictionary must be in place before the SIAM model is operational, as it supports the exchange of data and information across the SIAM ecosystem.

The need for a common data dictionary must be part of the tooling strategy, as the selected toolsets must be able to support its use.

7. SIAM Cultural Considerations

The SIAM ecosystem and the relationships between the customer organization, service integrator and service providers create a unique environment. From sourcing and contractual negotiations through to governance and operational management, there are specific SIAM considerations.

The cultural aspects of a transition to SIAM are one such consideration. An effective SIAM ecosystem is underpinned by effective relationships and appropriate behaviours. The ecosystem culture needs to encourage and reinforce these relationships and behaviours.

SIAM is often described as a sourcing strategy, but it is more than this. It extends beyond sourcing into the ongoing management and improvement of the service to deliver better business outcomes.

Service providers that compete in other areas of a market may find themselves working together to meet overall customer objectives in a SIAM ecosystem. Some service providers might be internal departments of the customer organization, working together with external service providers.

There are specific challenges when an external organization is fulfilling the service integrator role, because they are governing service providers who may also be their competitors.

The cultural considerations examined in this section are:
- Cultural change
- Collaboration and cooperation
- Cross-service provider organization.

7.1. Cultural Change

7.1.1. What does this mean in a SIAM Environment?

An organization that moves from either an insourced or a traditional outsourced environment to an environment based on SIAM will undergo a large program of change and transformation. If the cultural aspects of the change are not managed effectively, it can create disruption in the customer organization.

Adopting a new SIAM structure can include internal role changes in the customer organization, and staff being transferred from the customer organization to the service providers or the service integrator. This can have a significant impact on staff at a personal level; they will be concerned about their role, their career and their skillsets.

Moving to an environment that includes multiple service providers will require the customer organization to build SIAM expertise and capabilities, understanding of the ecosystem and technical landscape and the future technical roadmap and strategy. This expertise and knowledge might already exist in the organization, but in many transitions to SIAM it does not. Staff will need commercial, contractual and supplier management skills, in addition to more traditional service management skills.

Cultural change will also come from a change of management style. The customer organization needs to manage service provider performance at an executive, not an operational level. Its role is to step in and resolve contractual issues when required and to provide corporate governance. This is a shift away from managing activities to managing outcomes; in other words, managing the 'what', not the 'how'.

The customer organization needs to empower its service integrator to manage the service providers at the operational level. These changes in relationship dynamics and responsibilities will lead to, and depend on, changes in culture.

For the service providers, culture change is driven by the need to work collaboratively. All the service providers need to work with the service integrator and with other service providers towards their shared goal.

7.1.2. Why is it Important?

No organizational change can succeed without cultural change. If the culture and organizational behaviours stay the same, new processes and ways of working will not be adopted and expected benefits will not be delivered.

Effective management of cultural change will provide the basis for a successful SIAM transformation program, and will help the customer to retain skilled and motivated staff in key roles.

7.1.3. What Challenges will be Faced?

Some of the challenges related to cultural change are:
- Staff who are moving to a new organization can experience concern at a professional and at a personal, emotional level. Professionally, there will be a level of uncertainty over their role and their skills, and emotionally, they will be concerned about the impact on their life and career. This can lead to staff leaving, absenteeism and loyalty issues
- Organizations can suffer from change fatigue if too much is happening at once, leading to a higher chance of changes failing and new behaviours being not being adopted
- People continue using old processes or move back to old ways of working. It is important for every stakeholder in the SIAM ecosystem to reinforce behaviours; for example, at the service provider level, staff need to be encouraged to contact the service integrator, and not the customer
- The customer organization's own business outcomes may be negatively affected if the changes are disruptive and have an impact on service delivery.

7.1.4. How can they be Resolved?

These cultural issues can be addressed in several ways, including:
- Having a clear definition of the SIAM model and all associated roles and responsibilities at organization, team and individual levels
- From the customer perspective:

- Implementing a good business change or organizational change management process, reinforced with a strong communication plan to prevent misinformation and rumours spreading
- Applying program management to the SIAM roadmap, tracking progress and identifying where course corrections are needed to help increase confidence in likely success
- Considering the use of external consultancy to provide guidance, advice, and an objective view
- Understanding what retained capabilities are needed and putting plans in place to keep the skilled people in their roles
- From the customer and service integrator perspective, implementing a strong overarching governance structure, supported by processes which work in practice and not just in theory
- From the service integrator and service provider perspective, aligning their own communication plans with the overall communication plan and measuring the effectiveness of communication
- From a service provider perspective, understanding the organizations it will be working with, how they want to work together, and committing to the level of collaboration required in a SIAM environment.

7.1.5. Cultural change and the SIAM Structures

Externally sourced	▪ The key challenge for this structure relates to staff who are moving from the customer organization to another organization as part of the transition to SIAM; the professional and personal impact will need to be managed
Internally sourced	▪ To deliver effective cultural change and a successful transition to SIAM, the customer organization will need skilled people. These may not exist within the organization and could be difficult to recruit
Lead supplier	▪ As with the externally sourced service integrator structure, the key challenge for this structure relates to staff who are moving from the customer organization to another organization as part of the transition to SIAM; the professional and personal impact will need to be managed
Hybrid	▪ The key challenge for this structure is that confusion about roles and responsibilities can make it difficult for staff from the customer organization to change their behaviour; this applies if the interfaces between the customer and external organization at the service integrator level are not clearly defined. Staff need to be clear on their role and the role of the service integrator's employees.

7.2. Collaboration and Cooperation

7.2.1. What does this mean in a SIAM Ecosystem?

In many cases, a transition to SIAM means that service providers that are used to competing must work together to deliver customer outcomes. This often requires a change in mindset. The service providers must work together; the relationship moves from competitive to collaborative.

In an outsourced environment with no service integration element, service providers may pursue their own objectives. Silos and blame culture are commonplace. Within a SIAM ecosystem, the focus is on relationships, particularly cross-provider relationships, governance controls, and pursuit of common goals rather than achievement of specific individual organizational service levels and objectives.

In a SIAM ecosystem, service providers need to put competitive considerations aside and adapt to a new way of working. The customer and the service integrator also need to be clear on their role and the boundaries of their responsibilities. These organizations are also likely to be working in new ways.

Cultural considerations for collaboration and cooperation include:
- Fix first, argue later: when there is an issue affecting service, the service providers need to work together rather than assign blame or pass issues around
- Service providers must acknowledge that the service integrator is the voice of the customer, and has the autonomy to direct and make decisions and govern without being undermined
- From the customer's perspective, it needs to empower the service integrator to manage the service providers, and not interfere or duplicate effort
- Creating an environment that is focused on business outcomes and the customer, not individual service provider's contracts and agreements.

7.2.2. Why is it Important?

In a SIAM ecosystem, the service integrator does not usually have a contractual relationship with the service providers, but it does need to be able to manage and govern their behaviour on behalf of the customer.

If the parties in the ecosystem are not prepared to collaborate, the service integrator will not be able to control service delivery effectively.

For example, it will be very challenging for the service integrator to manage a major incident from end to end and within service targets if the service providers will not provide information or accept responsibility for investigation.

7.2.3. What Challenges will be Faced?

Some of the challenges related to collaboration and cooperation include:

- From the service integrator's perspective, the challenge of service providers bypassing it and going straight to the customer. The customer needs to support the service integrator by reinforcing correct communication paths, and the service integrator needs to build relationships and reiterate correct ways of working
- From the service provider's perspective:
    - 'Fix first argue later' being abused so that it incurs additional costs. This can happen if issues are identified and not corrected by the customer or the service integrator, so that the service provider must deal with them repeatedly
    - Being reluctant to collaborate and share with the other service providers
- Trust is a critical success factor for collaboration and cooperation. Trust between service providers (some of which may be internal, and some external), trust between the service providers and the service integrator, and trust between the service integrator and the customer must be built and maintained
- In a SIAM ecosystem that includes internal and external service providers, the internal service providers are part of the same organization as the customer. They may be reluctant to collaborate with the service integrator and with the external service providers; they may also have less mature delivery capabilities and so are less able to cooperate
- In a SIAM ecosystem that includes internal and external service providers, the internal service providers will not have the same contractual imperatives that require them to collaborate.

7.2.4. How can they be Resolved?

These cultural issues can be addressed in several ways, including:
- For all parties:
    - Creating a 'code of conduct' or 'rules of the club' agreement, with input from all parties in the SIAM ecosystem. These govern behaviours on a day to day basis; for example: how staff will behave in meetings, they will maintain professional and courteous behaviour always and will attend forums and make effective contributions. (see Section 8.2.4.1)
    - Signing collaboration agreements that are part of each contract, or agreed between parties after the contract is signed, to add more detail about how they will work together (see Section 8.2.4.2)
- Between the service integrator and each of the service providers, use operational level agreements (OLAs) to break down service targets and agreements into more detail, helping them to understand their role and their interfaces with other parts of the ecosystem, and when collaboration and cooperation is required (see Section 8.2.4.3).

7.2.4.1. *Example Code of Conduct*

A code of conduct (or 'rules of the club') document is not a contractual agreement. It provides high-level guidance for how the parties in the SIAM ecosystem will work together. All the parties can then hold each other to account, for example, highlighting if someone is behaving unacceptably in a meeting.

This will not usually be a formal document, and is normally quite brief, often only a single page. Where required, it may also include:
- Title page
- Document control: author, date, status, version, change log etc.
- Contents
- Introduction and document purpose
- Parties to the document
- Validity
- Approval/signatories.

The suggested key content is:

Partnership Aims
- What are the expected business outcomes?
- What is the SIAM ecosystem meant to deliver?

For example:
- Better value for money
- Greater efficiency and cost-effectiveness
- Greater flexibility to respond to evolving business requirements.

Partnership Ethos
- What values do the parties need to uphold?

For example:
- Maintain professionalism
- Work together as one team
- Share knowledge and ideas
- Embrace change
- Put the customer first
- Be courteous/respectful to others.

7.2.4.2. Example Collaboration Agreement

An effective collaboration agreement will help to create a culture based on working together to deliver shared outcomes, without continual reference back to contracts.

Collaboration agreements should be used with care. They should set out the intent of how service providers are expected to collaborate with each other, and with the service integrator.

Sufficient detail should be included to avoid ambiguity, and to reduce the likelihood of future disputes when a service provider was not aware of a specific collaboration requirement; for example, the need to take an active role in process forums.

Consideration must be given to the remedial approach that will be used if one of the parties does not align with the collaboration agreement.

This can form part of the contract with the customer but, to be truly effective, the parties should embrace the collaboration agreement as part of the SIAM culture, and not see it as a contractual requirement.

A typical collaboration agreement will contain the following sections:
- Title page
- Document control: author, date, status, version, change log etc.
- Contents
- Introduction
- Document purpose
- Parties to the document
- Validity period
- Termination
- Required behaviours: for example, avoid unnecessary duplication of effort, do not hinder or withhold information from other service providers
- Mechanisms to support collaboration: for example, commitment to support process forums to review, improve and innovate processes and service delivery; commitment to triage and work together to resolve issues/challenges when requested by the service integrator; commitment to be involved in reviews and assurance activities
- Where relevant, toolsets to support collaboration
- Expected areas of collaboration: for example, review of proposed changes, incident investigation, taking part in working groups, innovation
- Dependencies between parties
- Any non-financial/non-contractual remedies: for example, where one or more service providers agrees with the service integrator and the customer to carry out actions to address an issue rather than trigger a contractual target and accept a financial penalty
- Change control
- Dispute resolution and escalation points.

7.2.4.3. Example Operational Level Agreement

Operational level agreements (OLA) between the service integrator and a service provider break down service targets into more detail.

They support end to end service delivery. For example, end to end incident management might include a four-hour resolution time for priority one incidents. In the OLA, the service provider might agree to a target of 30 minutes to either accept an incident or pass the information to a different service provider.

Within a SIAM ecosystem, it is important to define each service and its associated targets fully. OLAs support that definition and provide control and visibility.

OLAs are prepared by the service integrator with input from the service providers. The service provider referenced in the OLA must have agreed the contents. The OLA supports the overall customer objectives, but the customer may not be interested in the document detail.

An operational level agreement should include content such as:
- Title page
- Document control: author, date, status, version, change log etc.
- Contents
- Introduction
- Document purpose
- Parties to the document
- Validity
- Approval/signatories
- Rules for OLA termination
- Rules for OLA governance and escalation criteria
- Review schedule
- OLA change management
- Service description
- Scope of OLA: in- and out-of-scope activities
- Dependent services
- OLA details:
  - Name of service (e.g. service desk, capacity management)

- Service description
- Service hours
- Service provider
- Service consumers
- Service outcomes
- Contact points and roles
- Agreed activities of all parties (e.g. party A will send an incident record to party B, party B will confirm receipt)
- Service targets
- Measurement: availability, performance targets etc.
- RACI matrix
  - Service boundaries
  - Quality assurance and service reporting
  - Service reviews
  - Glossary.

7.2.5. Collaboration and Cooperation and the SIAM Structures

Externally sourced	- Internal service providers may be unwilling to collaborate and cooperate with the external service integrator
Internally sourced	- External service providers may be more willing to collaborate and cooperate as it will perceive the service integrator as the customer
- There is a risk that a customer organization might not manage the service providers well owing to a lack of SIAM experience. If the service integrator cannot encourage the right culture and behaviours, this will affect the level of collaboration and cooperation
- If the internal service integrator is seen to treat internal service providers differently this can lead to reduced collaboration and cooperation by the external service providers
- Internal service providers may be unwilling to collaborate and cooperate with the internal service integrator

Lead supplier	- Internal service providers may be unwilling to collaborate and cooperate with the external service integrator
- If the lead supplier is seen to favor its own service provider in its service integrator role, this can lead to reduced collaboration and cooperation from the other service providers
Hybrid	- The roles and responsibilities of the customer acting as service integrator and the third-party service integrator need to be clear. It is challenging for service providers to collaborate if they do not understand the structure and boundaries of responsibilities
- Internal service providers may be unwilling to collaborate and cooperate with the hybrid service integrator because it includes external elements.

7.3. Cross-service Provider Organization

This section addresses the cultural aspects of cross-service provider organization only. For more detail about managing cross-functional teams and managing conflict see Section 6.1: People Practices.

Cross-service provider organization describes the cultural considerations associated with managing a service across multiple service providers.

7.3.1. What does this mean in a SIAM Ecosystem?

The SIAM ecosystem can include an internal, hybrid, external, or lead supplier service integrator, plus several internal or external service providers.

Each service provider will have its own strategies, objectives and ways of working. The customer organization does not always have the ability (or desire) to mandate that all service providers follow a common set of processes or use the same toolset. They do, however, require all service providers to be able to interface with and integrate into the end to end service management processes.

From a cultural perspective, cross-service provider organization requires service providers to have appropriate behaviours and attitudes to support the customer organization and help them achieve its goals, rather than focusing on individual goals.

7.3.2. Why is it Important?

Successful cross-service provider organization supports delivery of the end to end service. It starts with the customer organization. The customer needs to articulate a clear vision of what success looks like to all the service providers in the SIAM ecosystem.

The vision needs to be cascaded through all layers and across the ecosystem. This will then enable consistent:

- Strategies
- Objectives
- Processes; this does not preclude service providers using their own processes and procedures, but ensures that the overall end to end process is integrated, can be managed, and is driving the correct outcomes.

7.3.3. What Challenges will be faced?

Some of the cultural challenges related to cross-service provider organization include:

- The customer retained organization may step back into its old role and get involved with delivery, rather than focusing on corporate governance and its own business objectives. This creates confusion, duplication and does not allow the service providers, the service integrator, or the customer to work effectively
- Service providers focus on their own targets at the expense of end to end service targets
- Service providers do not buy into the culture of collaboration and do not share innovations and potential improvements with other parts of the ecosystem
- The service integrator does not treat service providers equally, leading to resentment and disengagement

- If service providers have poor interfaces with end to end service management processes and tools, the role of the service integrator becomes more challenging; for example, monitoring, reporting, measurement will all be less effective.

7.3.4. How can they be Resolved?

These cultural issues can be addressed in several ways, including:
- For all parties:
    - Establishing consistent contractual targets/service level agreements and common performance measures/key performance indicators across the supply chain, so that all service providers feel they are equal and not disadvantaged
    - Having performance measures that encourage partnering and shared innovation with other parties
    - Cross-service provider processes must be based on a common language that all parties can understand
- From the customer perspective, empowering the service integrator to have ownership, responsibility and accountability
- From the customer, service integrator, and service provider perspective, celebrate success, praise excellent service performance, delivery and innovation, to emphasize and reward the desired behaviours
- Establish 'champion' process forums with representation from the service integrator and all service providers to discuss and improve the effectiveness of end to end processes, tools, interfaces and integration.

7.3.5. Cross-service Provider Organization and the SIAM Structures

Externally sourced	• External service providers may be reluctant to share information about how they work with an external service integrator, if they view them as a competitor
Internally sourced	• Internal service providers may be unwilling to work with and integrate with external service providers
Lead supplier	• The external organization that is acting as the service integrator and a service provider could be

	seen as a 'favourite' of the customer. If other service providers don't feel they are being treated fairly, they are less likely to work together
Hybrid	- Effective cross-service provider organization requires clear direction from the customer and the service integrator. If the roles within the hybrid service integrator are not clearly defined, meetings and structures to support cross-service provider organization may not be put in place.

8. Challenges and Risks

Adopting a SIAM model requires an organizational transformation. The changes that are involved will affect people, processes, technology; and the interfaces between them.

As with any organizational change, there will be challenges to face. These challenges can have a significant impact on the transition to a SIAM model and will require concerted effort to overcome.

Each challenge has associated risks, which need to be recorded, evaluated, managed and mitigated (where appropriate) using a risk management methodology. The impact of the challenge and associated risks will influence the amount of time and resources that will be used to address them.

The challenges and risks described here should be considered by any organization planning to adopt SIAM. They may not all be relevant, but can provide useful input for SIAM planning.

8.1. Challenge: Building the Business Case

Organizations must be clear about their business case for SIAM. This should include the expected benefits and costs.

It is not always possible to have a complete picture during the Discovery and Strategy stage of the roadmap, as some of the detail may not be known until the Plan and Build stage. However, it is usual to create an outline business case before starting a SIAM implementation that will be developed throughout the SIAM roadmap into a full business case.

The business case should include the drivers that apply to the organization, drawn from the five SIAM driver groups (documented in Section 1.5.2: Drivers for SIAM):
1. Service satisfaction
2. Service and sourcing landscape
3. Operational efficiencies

4. External drivers
5. Commercial drivers.

The business case also needs to articulate the benefits that the organization expects to achieve by adopting a SIAM model. These could include, for example:
- Mitigating the risk of procuring services from a single provider by leveraging best of breed services from several providers
- Improving their capability to add and remove service providers
- Improving the quality of service
- Increasing the value derived from IT services.

These benefits will only be achieved though clear objectives, robust planning, and effective management.

8.1.1. Which Parties will this Challenge Affect?

This challenge mainly applies to the customer that is creating the business case. It can also apply to an organization that intends to be an external service integrator, as it will need to be able to justify the cost of its services.

8.1.2. Which Roadmap Stage will this Challenge Affect?

This challenge starts early in the SIAM roadmap, during Discovery and Strategy, and continues all the way through.

At the end of the Discovery and Strategy stage, executive backing is required to approve the outline business case for SIAM, and to allocate resources to the next stage.

At the end of the Plan and Build stage, executive backing is required to authorize any procurements and allocate resources to the remaining stages. The business case will also be used during the Implement and Run and Improve stages to verify that the anticipated benefits are being realised.

8.1.3. Associated Risks
Without a strong business case, there are several risks, including:
- The customer organization's executives do not approve the transition to SIAM
- The customer organization's executives approve the transition to SIAM, but do not allocate enough resources or provide sufficient support
- The customer organization starts the transformation process without a clear picture of the benefits it expects to achieve; this will make it difficult to verify if the transition to SIAM has been successful
- The success of the program cannot be measured because anticipated benefits have not been clearly defined
- The costs of the transition to SIAM are understated, so there may not be enough budget available to complete the transition.

8.1.4. Potential Mitigation
These risks can be mitigated by:
- Allocating skilled resources to build the business case
- Executing all the activities in the Discovery and Strategy and Plan and Build stages
- Linking the strategy for SIAM to the customer organization's high-level strategy and objectives
- Identifying and addressing each of the appropriate drivers for the SIAM transformation
- Adding as much detail as possible and refining the business case as the roadmap proceeds
- Identifying any current contracts that are inefficient
- Identifying contracts that are providing good value and are a good cultural fit
- Using industry data/benchmarks where available to show the benefits of SIAM in other organizations
- Including the proposed SIAM structure and SIAM model
- Documenting the expected benefits.

8.2. Challenge: Level of Control and Ownership

During the Discovery and Strategy stage of the roadmap, the customer organization needs to consider how it will balance the level of control it wants to have over service provision, processes, tools and data against the benefits it will obtain from delegating them to a service integrator. This decision is then confirmed in the Plan and Build stage.

8.2.1. Which Parties will this Challenge Affect?

This challenge mainly applies to the customer organization while it decides on its preferred SIAM structure and model, and sets policies related to roles, responsibilities, data and tooling.

If this challenge is not resolved, it can make the definition of the SIAM model, and the role of the service integrator and the service providers, more challenging because responsibilities and accountabilities are unclear.

8.2.2. Which Roadmap Stage will this Challenge Affect?

The level of control and ownership needs to be decided at a high-level during Discovery and Strategy, and more detail added during Plan and Build.

8.2.3. Associated Risks

If the level of control and ownership is not clearly defined, associated risks include:
- If the customer is not prepared to relinquish ownership of service activities and processes, it may not be possible to realize the anticipated benefits from SIAM, as the service integrator may be unable to perform its role
- If the customer relinquishes all control and accountability, the service integrator might not have enough strategic direction to allow it to carry out its role
- If the level of control associated with data is too restrictive, the service integrator and service providers may not have access to the data they need
- If the level of control associated with data is not restrictive enough, the customer's data may be at risk, for example from a security breach

- If the ownership of data is not defined, the customer might find it no longer has access to data about, for example, incident and change records related to its services.

8.2.4. Potential Mitigation

These risks can be mitigated by:
- Defining a clear vision and selecting an appropriate SIAM structure and SIAM model during the Discovery and Strategy, and Plan and Build stages of the roadmap
- Ensuring that the customer organization understands the difference between governance and management, so it is clear what activities it needs to monitor, and what it needs to do. This will form part of the governance framework
- Implementing clear policies for data, tooling and processes
- Defining ownership of processes, tools, data, information and knowledge during the Plan and Build stage of the SIAM roadmap.

8.3. Challenge: Legacy Contracts

There are two main challenges associated with legacy contracts:

- Not fit for purpose: some legacy contracts might still be in place after the SIAM implementation. The contractual requirements in the legacy contract with the service provider are unlikely to align with the new SIAM model
- Expiry: continuity of service may be compromised if legacy service provider contracts expire before the implementation of new service provider contracts.

It is important to recognize that service providers who are not going to be part of the future operating model may be challenging to deal with.

8.3.1. Which Parties will this Challenge Affect?

This challenge will affect the customer that owns the SIAM model, and the service integrator that will be coordinating the services. The existing service providers will be affected; as will new service providers being added.

8.3.2. Which Roadmap Stage will this Challenge Affect?

Contracts that may not be fit for purpose should be identified during the Discovery and Strategy roadmap stage. If no action is taken during Plan and Build, the effects will be felt during the rest of the SIAM implementation and delivery.

Contract expiry will affect the Plan and Build stage, and can also affect the Implement stage.

8.3.3. Associated Risks

The potential risks associated with legacy contracts include:

- Increased service integrator workload, when unexpired legacy contracts need to be integrated into the SIAM model
- A gap in service if a legacy contract expires before a new SIAM-based contract is in place
- Additional customer costs for extensions to existing contracts during the transition to SIAM, or for early release from an existing contract.

8.3.4. Potential Mitigation

Risks associated with contracts not being fit for purpose can be mitigated by:

- Understanding which contracts this relates to and creating a timetable to show how long the risk will exist for
- Sharing the new SIAM vision with the existing service providers
- Renegotiating/amending contracts where possible; it is possible that requirements, SLAs, and measurements could be changed
- Investigating the cost of termination
- Creating a contingency plan if the contract cannot be amended or terminated
- Using the information to guide the design approach taken in Plan and Build
- Creating a mechanism for the service integrator to report any issues related to existing contracts.

Risks associated with contracts expiring can be mitigated by:
- Developing a clear understanding of all existing service provider contracts so there are no surprises
- Developing a roadmap for the transition to SIAM that aligns with existing expiry dates as far as possible
- Creating contingency plans in case of delays
- Negotiating extension options with existing service providers.

8.4. Challenge: Commercial Challenges

Commercial challenges relate to how the SIAM model is established and the structure that is chosen. The customer, the service integrator and the service providers all need to feel they are getting what they expect and are being treated fairly.

If a customer organization does not have mature SIAM capabilities, the commercial agreements it puts in place may not be appropriate.

8.4.1. Which Parties will this Challenge Affect?

All the parties in the SIAM ecosystem can be affected by this challenge:

- The customer needs to feel they are getting value for money
- Externally sourced service integrators and all service providers need to be profitable and not incur penalties they see as unfair
- The service integrator and the customer need to have an appropriate commercial framework to govern and incentivise the service providers.

8.4.2. Which Roadmap Stage will this Challenge Affect?

This challenge will span the entire roadmap. Commercial decisions will be made during Discovery and Strategy, and then detail will be added and contracts defined during Plan and Build. They need to be monitored during Implement, and Run and Improve activities identified where necessary.

8.4.3. Associated Risks

Commercial risks include:

- Unrealistic targets and service levels for service providers may result in their withdrawing from the ecosystem

- Lack of clearly defined boundaries between service providers make it challenging to allocate responsibility for service failures
- The service integrator is managing the service providers from a SIAM perspective but does not have any direct contracts with them; unless the right level of empowerment is in place, the service integrator may not be effective
- The service providers impose their own contracts that have targets that do not align with end to end service requirements (for example, when the service provider is a very large organization it may have a standard set of service levels).

8.4.4. Potential Mitigation

These risks can be mitigated by:

- Getting the right skills and experience involved during contractual negotiations
- Defining service boundaries and service interactions
- Including in service provider contracts that the service integrator is the managing agent of the customer, with devolved authority for managing delivery against contracts
- Making sure targets and service levels flow down and are apportioned across service providers
- Ensuring that penalties and service credits can be calculated correctly
- Having clear and unambiguous contracts
- Scheduling regular reviews to assess if contracts are performing as they should.

8.5. Challenge: Security

Implementing a SIAM model requires sharing of data and information about services across multiple service providers. Security needs to be embedded in every layer, through roles, responsibilities, communication and reporting.

The customer organization needs to be clear about what data and information exists in the ecosystem, where it is, and how it will be managed and secured.

8.5.1. Which Parties will this Challenge Affect?

This challenge affects the customer, the service integrator and the service providers; each party has a responsibility for the overall security of the service.

8.5.2. Which Roadmap Stage will this Challenge Affect?

If security related roles and activities are not clearly defined during Plan and Build, the impact will be felt in later roadmap stages.

In a worst-case scenario, a security incident during 'Run' might take longer to discover because no one party is responsible for detecting it. The response could also be slow because the service providers do not have clarity on individual responsibilities.

8.5.3. Associated Risks

Potential risks associated with security include:

- A lack of understanding of the customer organization's legislative and regulatory responsibilities, and a lack of education for the service integrator and service providers to make them aware of these
- A lack of understanding of the criticality of information, and no agreed approach to managing information
- Inability to map dataflows and the end to end service, to identify what is in scope for security
- Security roles and responsibilities not mapped and allocated
- Process inadequacies, including a lack of access management for service providers to ensure they can only access what is necessary
- Ineffective data segregation, particularly in relation to a service provider's commercially sensitive data that should not be visible to other service providers
- If roles are not clear security tasks might be duplicated, leading to wasted effort, or not managed, leading to service unavailability and security breaches.

8.5.4. Potential Mitigation

These risks can be mitigated by:

- Having a clear security strategy and supporting policies that are cascaded to all service providers via the service integrator
- Using other practices like COBIT® and OBASHI to help identify information assets and dataflows
- Designing and implementing end to end security management
- Implementing effective processes such as access management
- Identifying and completing security activities when adding and removing service providers; service providers being added need enough access to be effective, and service providers that are being removed need to have access terminated
- Creating a schedule for audits and testing
- Encouraging a culture of openness so service providers are confident to share information about a breach
- Establishing a process forum for security.

8.6. Challenge: Cultural Fit

Different service providers will have different corporate cultures, which all need to work within the SIAM ecosystem.

Service providers need to work together to meet customer outcomes, often with organizations with whom they are in competition in the broader marketplace.

Existing service providers might not be willing to change to adapt to the SIAM model. New service providers need to be a good cultural fit.

8.6.1. Which Parties will this Challenge Affect?

This challenge affects the customer, the service integrator and the service providers; each party has a role to play in cultural change.

8.6.2. Which Roadmap Stage will this Challenge Affect?

This challenge needs to be initially addressed in Plan and Build. The issues will increase during the Implement stage, and may worsen during Run and Improve.

8.6.3. Associated Risks

Potential risks associated with cultural fit include:

- Service providers not working well together
- Service providers not interacting with end to end processes and procedures
- End to end service targets not being met
- Cultural issues can lead to SIAM benefits not being delivered to the customer organization
- The service integrator being unable to fulfil their role because the service providers are not working together
- Frustration for all parties if a service provider says one thing and does another.

8.6.4. Potential Mitigation

These risks can be mitigated by:
- Being aware of the risk of cultural mismatch, and planning to identify it and intervene where required
- Assessing cultural fit during procurement and selecting service providers who will be a good cultural fit
- Encouraging a culture of collaboration
- Using collaboration agreements (see Section 7.2.4)
- Demonstrating correct behaviour at the customer and service integrator level
- Establishing SIAM structural elements (boards, forums and working groups) to build relationships and reinforce culture.

8.7. Challenge: Behaviours

When a major organizational change happens, it is easy and tempting for staff to revert to old ways of working with which they are more familiar.

This might mean that the intended value of the SIAM implementation is not realized, because the implementation does not become 'business as usual' or an accepted way of working. An effective SIAM ecosystem relies on much more than just contractual agreements. It also relies on good relationships between the customer, the service integrator and the service providers.

8.7.1. Which Parties will this Challenge Affect?
This challenge affects the customer, the service integrator and the service providers; all parties must adopt new behaviours to make the SIAM model successful.

8.7.2. Which Roadmap Stage will this Challenge Affect?
This will typically happen during Run and Improve, but also during the Implement stage.

In the Implement stage, SIAM is the new way of working and all parties must work together to implement the SIAM model. In Run and Improve, it needs to become 'business as usual'. Behaviour needs to be reviewed continually, and revisited if key staff change or a new service provider is added.

8.7.3. Associated Risks
Potential risks associated with behaviour include:

- Service provider staff circumventing the service integrator to talk directly to the customer, and vice versa
- One or more service providers not engaging fully
- The service integrator is perceived as being biased
- The customer service integrator acts in a dictatorial way and does not have good relationships with the service providers
- The customer and the service integrator don't present a united front
- Relationships become reliant on key personnel, who could leave
- Failure to achieve service levels.

8.7.4. Potential Mitigation

These risks can be mitigated by:

- Continual reinforcement of correct behaviour at all levels
- The customer and the service integrator presenting a united front to service providers
- Regular behaviour reviews and audits
- Ongoing training and awareness for staff
- Use of collaboration agreements (see Section 7.2.4)
- Providing regular communication to build relationships, based on a communication plan that identifies relevant stakeholder groups and describes a communication strategy for each of them
- All the involved parties holding each other accountable for their behaviour
- The customer and service integrator being realistic about what can be achieved; working with service providers - not punishing them
- Implementation of the SIAM structural elements
- Rewarding good behaviours.

8.8. Challenge: Measuring Success

To show that SIAM is delivering value, it must be measured. Developing an end to end performance management and reporting framework that spans multiple service providers can be a significant challenge.

8.8.1. Which Parties will this Challenge Affect?

This challenge will affect the customer if it is unable to validate whether SIAM is delivering value and services are performing, and the service integrator that has the task of building the end to end reports.

8.8.2. Which Roadmap Stage will this Challenge Affect?

This challenge will usually happen during Run and Improve, when the customer tries to measure the effectiveness of SIAM in the business as usual environment.

The measures should be defined during Plan and Build, linked to the original drivers for SIAM identified in Discovery and Strategy.

Measurements will need to evolve when improvement activities take place.

8.8.3. Associated Risks

Potential risks associated with measuring success include:

- Measures not aligned with the anticipated benefits from the business case
- Not measuring and reporting on the right things
- Measuring too much, which wastes resources and can obscure important information
- Not measuring enough to identify the required information
- Being unable to measure services from end to end.

8.8.4. Potential Mitigation

These risks can be mitigated by:

- Creating an effective performance management and reporting framework
- Clearly defining who needs to measure what, when, how and why
- Regularly reviewing reports to confirm they are still fit for purpose
- Using a mix of qualitative and quantitative measures.

8.9. Challenge: Trust/Eliminating Micro-management

Trust between all parties is essential in SIAM ecosystems.

A lack of trust can manifest itself as duplication of roles and activities, such as the customer continually checking what the service integrator has done. The customer organization might be unable to let go of activities it used to perform.

It can also result in micro-management, for example, the service integrator reviewing every aspect of every change from the service providers.

All of this will increase cost, leading to savings and efficiencies not being realized. It can also cause confusion and inconsistency.

8.9.1. Which Parties will this Challenge Affect?

Lack of trust and micro-management can affect the customer organization, the service integrator and the service providers.

8.9.2. Which Roadmap Stage will this Challenge Affect?

This challenge will usually be identified after SIAM has become business as usual, so in the Implement and Run and Improve roadmap stages. To address it, mitigating activities and plans should begin in the Plan and Build stage.

8.9.3. Associated Risks

Potential risks associated with lack of trust and micro-management between the customer and service integrator include:

- The customer has a larger than needed retained organization
- The customer organization won't realize any benefits from adopting SIAM, because it continues to work as it always has done
- Process and service activities are duplicated by the customer and the service integrator
- The customer organization wastes time and resources micro-managing and checking the work of the service integrator
- The service integrator wastes time and resources providing extra, unnecessary customer reports
- The service providers continue to interact directly with the customer, because they see the customer does not value the service integrator.

Potential risks associated with lack of trust and micro-management between the service integrator and service providers include:

- Process and service activities are being duplicated by the service integrator and the service providers
- The service integrator wastes time and resources micro-managing and checking the work of the service providers
- The service providers waste time and resources providing extra, unnecessary reports
- The service providers continue to interact directly with the customer, because they do not value the service integrator.

8.9.4. Potential Mitigation

These risks can be mitigated by:

- Careful design of the SIAM model in the Plan and Build stage, particularly roles, responsibilities, and governance framework
- Adopting a phased approach to the implementation of SIAM to allow the customer to develop trust in the service integrator
- Having regular communication and a culture of improvement to identify and discuss micro-management and duplication of effort
- Establishing effective structural elements to support relationships and build trust.

Appendix A: Glossary of Terms

This glossary defines the terms used in this document. This includes the specific SIAM definitions for common terms such as 'board'.

Aggregation	Also referred to as service aggregation. Bringing together components and elements to create a group (or service)
Board	Boards perform governance in the SIAM ecosystem. They are formal decision making bodies, and are accountable for the decisions that they take. Boards are a type of structural element
Business as usual (BAU)	The normal state of something
Business case	Outlines a proposed course of action, its potential costs and benefits. Supports decision making
Capability	The power or ability to do something[21]
Cloud services	Services that are provided over the internet, including software as a service (SaaS), infrastructure as a service (IaaS) and platform as a service (PaaS). Often treated as a commodity service
COBIT®	COBIT® (Control Objectives for Information and Related Technologies) is a framework for IT governance and management created by ISACA
Code of conduct	A code of conduct (or 'rules of the club') document is not a contractual agreement. It provides high-level guidance for how the parties in the SIAM ecosystem will work together
Collaboration agreement	A collaboration agreement helps to create a culture based on working together to deliver shared outcomes, without continual reference back to contracts
Commodity service	A service that can easily be replaced; for example, internet hosting is often a commodity service
Contract	An agreement between two legal entities. SIAM contracts are often shorter in duration than traditional outsourcing contracts, and have targets to drive collaborative behaviour and innovation
Customer (organization)	The customer organization is the end client who is making the transition to SIAM as part of its operating model. It commissions the SIAM ecosystem
Disaggregation	Splitting a group into component parts
Ecosystem	The SIAM ecosystem includes three layers: customer organization (including retained capabilities), service integrator, and service provider(s)
Enterprise architecture	A definition of the structure and operation of an organization. It maps the current state and can be used to support planning for desired future states
Enterprise service bus	A type of 'middleware' that provides services to link more complex architectures
External service provider	An external service provider is an organization that provides services and is not part of the customer organization. It is a separate legal entity

---

[21] Oxford English Dictionary © 2016 Oxford University Press

Externally sourced service integrator	Type of SIAM structure: the customer appoints an external organization to take the role and provide the capabilities of the service integrator
Function	An organizational entity, typically characterized by a special area of knowledge or experience[22]
Governance	Governance refers to the rules, policies, processes (and in some cases, legislation) by which businesses are operated, regulated and controlled. There may be many layers of governance within a business from enterprise, corporate and IT. In a SIAM ecosystem, governance refers to the definition and application of policies and standards. These define and ensure the required levels of authority, decision making and accountability.
Governance framework	Within a SIAM ecosystem, allows the customer organization to exercise and maintain authority over the ecosystem. It includes corporate governance requirements, controls to be retained by the customer, governance structural elements, segregation of duties, and risk, performance, contract and dispute management approaches
Governance model	Designed based on the governance framework and roles and responsibilities. Includes scope, accountabilities, responsibilities, meeting formats and frequencies, inputs, outputs, hierarchy, terms of reference and related policies
Hybrid service integrator	Type of SIAM structure: the customer collaborates with an external organization to take the role of service integrator and provide the service integrator capability
Infrastructure as a Service (IaaS)	A type of cloud service that allows customers to access virtualized computing resources
Insourcing	Sourcing from within the organization
Intelligent client function	See retained capabilities
Internal service provider	An internal service provider is a team or department that is part of the customer organization. Its performance is typically managed using internal agreements and targets
Internally sourced service integrator	Type of SIAM structure: the customer organization takes the role of service integrator, providing the service integration capability
ITIL®	ITIL® is the most widely accepted approach to IT service management in the world, and is a registered trademark of AXELOS Limited
Key performance indicator (KPI)	A metric used to measure performance. KPIs are defined for services, processes and business objectives
Layers (SIAM layers)	There are three layers in the SIAM ecosystem: customer organization (including retained capabilities), service integrator, and service provider(s)
Lead supplier service integrator	Type of SIAM structure: the role of service integrator is taken by an external organization that is also an external service provider
Man-marking	An undesirable and wasteful type of micro-management, where the customer checks the work of the service integrator constantly
Management methodology	A management methodology describes methods, rules and principles associated with a discipline
Microsoft Operations Framework (MOF)	A guide for IT professionals that describes how to create, implement and manage services

---

[22] Source: IT Process Wiki

Model (SIAM model)	A customer organization develops its SIAM model based on the practices, processes, functions, roles and structural elements described within the SIAM methodology. Their model will be based on the layers in the SIAM ecosystem
Multi-sourcing	Sourcing of goods or services from more than one supplier
Multi-sourcing integration (MSI)	May be used as an acronym for SIAM
Open Systems Interconnect (OSI)	A reference model for how applications communicate over a network
Operational level agreement (OLA)	Within the SIAM context, OLAs are created between the service integrator and service providers to break down end to end service targets into detail and individual responsibilities
Organizational change management	The process used to manage changes to business processes, organizational structures and cultural changes within an organization
Outsourcing	Procuring goods or services from an external organization
Performance management and reporting framework	The performance management and reporting framework for SIAM addresses measuring and reporting on a range of items including: - Key performance indicators - Performance of processes and process models - Achievement of service level targets - System and service performance - Adherence to contractual and non-contractual responsibilities - Collaboration - Customer satisfaction
Platform as a Service (PaaS)	A type of cloud service that allows customers to use virtual platforms for their application development and management. This removes the need for them to build their own infrastructure
Practice	The actual application or use of an idea, belief, or method, as opposed to theories relating to it[23]
Prime vendor	A sourcing approach where the service provider sub-contracts to other service providers to deliver the service, and the customer only has a contractual relationship with the prime vendor
Process	A documented, repeatable approach to carrying out a series of tasks or activities
Process forum	Process forums are aligned to specific processes or practices. Their members work together on proactive development, innovations, and improvements. Forums will convene regularly, for as long as the SIAM model is in place. Process forums are a type of structural element
Process manager	Responsible for process execution
Process model	Describe the purpose and outcomes for a process, as well as activities, inputs, outputs, interactions, controls, measures and supporting policies and templates

---

[23] Source: Google

Process owner	A process owner is accountable for end to end process design and process performance
Program management	The process responsible for managing groups of projects to deliver a unified goal
Project management	A process that provides a repeatable approach to deliver successful projects
RACI	RACI is an acronym that stands for Responsible, Accountable, Consulted and Informed. These are the 4 key 'involvements' that can be assigned to an activity and a role. A RACI chart is a matrix of all the activities or decision making authorities undertaken in an organization set against all the people or roles
Request for information (RFI)	A business process used to compare suppliers, by collecting information about them and their capabilities
Request for proposal (RFP)	A business process used to allow suppliers to bid for a piece of work or project
Retained capability/capabilities	The customer organization will include some retained capabilities. The retained capabilities are the functions that are responsible for strategic, architectural, business engagement and corporate governance activities. The service integrator is independent from the retained capabilities, even if it is internally sourced. Service integration is not a retained capability. Retained capabilities are sometimes referred to as the 'intelligent client function'
Roadmap	The SIAM roadmap has four stages: Discovery and Strategy, Design and Build, Implement Run and Improve
Separation of duties/concerns	An internal control used to prevent errors or fraud, separate of duties defines what each role is authorized to do, and when more than one person must be involved in a task. For example, a developer might not be permitted to test and approve their own code
Service	A system that meets a need, for example, email is an 'IT service' that facilitates communication
Service boundaries	A definition of what parts make up a service (what is 'inside the boundary'), often used in technical architecture documents
Service consumer	The organization directly using the service
Service integration (SI)	May be used as an acronym for SIAM
Service integration and management (SIAM)	Service integration and management (SIAM) is a management methodology that can be applied in an environment that includes services sourced from a number of service providers. Sometimes referred to as SI&M
Service integrator	A single, logical entity held accountable for the end to end delivery of services and the business value that the customer receives. The service integrator is accountable for end to end service governance, management, integration, assurance and coordination
Service integrator layer	The service integrator layer of the SIAM ecosystem is where end to end service governance, management, integration, assurance and coordination is performed
Service management	The management practices and capabilities that an organization uses to provide services to consumers
Service management and integration (SMAI)	May be used as an acronym for SIAM
Service management integration (SMI)	May be used as an acronym for SIAM
Service manager	Responsible for service delivery for one or more services

Service model	A way of modelling the hierarchy of services, including services that are directly consumed by the customer organization and underpinning services and dependencies
Service orchestration	Service orchestration is the term used to define the end to end view of service activities and establishing the standards for inputs and outputs to the end to end process. This includes defining control mechanisms while still allowing service providers to define the mechanisms of fulfilment and the freedom to pursue internal processes
Service outcomes	A definition of what a service is meant to achieve or deliver
Service owner	A role that is accountable for the end to end performance of a service
Service provider	Within a SIAM ecosystem, there are multiple service providers. Each service provider is responsible for the delivery of one or more services, or service elements, to the customer. It is responsible for managing the products and technology used to deliver its contracted or agreed services, and operating its own processes. They can be internal or external to the customer organization. Historically referred to as towers, may also be referred to as vendors or suppliers
Service provider category	Service providers can be categorized as strategic, tactical or commodity.
Shadow IT	Shadow IT describes IT services and systems commissioned by business departments, without the knowledge of the IT department (sometimes referred to as 'stealth IT').
SIAM model	See model
SIAM structures	The four structures describe how the service integrator is sourced: internally, externally, from a lead supplier or as a hybrid
Software as a Service (SaaS)	A cloud service where software is paid for monthly as a subscription rather than purchased as a one-time payment
Sourcing	The procurement approach an organization adopts; for example, sourcing services internally or externally. Adopting SIAM will affect how an organization sources services and the types of contracts it puts in place with service providers
Structural element	Structural elements are teams that have members from different organizations and different SIAM layers. They include: boards, process forums and working groups
Supplier	An organization from whom the customer receives goods or services
Tooling strategy	Defines what tools will be used, who will own them, and how they will support the flow of data and information between the SIAM layers
Tower	See service provider
Watermelon effect (Watermelon reporting)	The watermelon effect occurs when a report is 'green on the outside, red on the inside'. The service provider(s) meet individual targets, but the end to end service is not meeting the customer's requirements
Working group	Working groups are convened to address specific issues or projects. They are typically formed on a reactive ad-hoc or fixed-term basis. They can include staff from different organizations and different specialist areas. Working groups are a structural element

Appendix B Process Guide

B.1 What is a Process

A process is *"a documented, repeatable approach to carrying out a series of tasks or activities"*

Most business activities involve repeated tasks; for example, taking a phone call from a customer, raising an invoice, or managing a complaint.

Documenting a process for a repeated task has several benefits:

- It allows the organization to define its preferred approach to managing the task
- The task will be carried out consistently
- It avoids staff wasting time recreating an approach each time the task is carried out
- New staff can be quickly trained to carry out a process
- It can be measured and assessed
- It can be used as a baseline for improvement.

A process takes one or more inputs, performs activities on them, and transforms them into one or more outputs.

A process description document will normally include:

- The purpose and objectives of the process
- The trigger for starting the process
- Process activities or steps
- Roles and responsibilities, including a RACI model
- Metrics for the process, including service levels, targets, and key performance indicators
- Process inputs and outputs
- Escalation paths
- Associated toolsets
- Data and information requirements.

Every process should have an owner. The owner is the single, accountable role that ensures the process is correctly defined, executed and reviewed. In larger organizations, process manager roles might also be part of the organizational structure; these roles are responsible for the execution of process activities.

For example, the process owner for change management might be the organization's change manager. They could be supported by a number of change analysts, who would be fulfilling process manager-type roles.

Processes are part of an organization's SIAM model.

This document describes some common processes at a high level, and also includes SIAM considerations to help organizations start to adapt processes within a SIAM ecosystem.

This is not an exhaustive list of processes used within SIAM ecosystems; neither is it an in-depth process guide for commonly used service management processes that are fully described in other management practices, frameworks and standards like ISO/IEC 20000.

B.2 Processes and the SIAM Ecosystem

SIAM itself is not a process; however, to operate effectively, it relies on a number of processes.

Most management approaches expect processes to be executed within one organization. Within a SIAM ecosystem, processes are likely to be executed:
- Across different organizations in the same SIAM layer
- Across organizations in different SIAM layers.

Processes need to be allocated to the appropriate layers in the SIAM model. This allocation may be different for each implementation of SIAM.

Many of the processes used within a SIAM ecosystem are processes familiar from other practices, for example, change management and business relationship management.

Within a SIAM model, these processes require adaptation and augmentation to support integration and coordination between the different parties involved. They also require alignment with other parts of the SIAM model including:
- SIAM practices
- SIAM layers
- Governance model
- Structural elements.

The execution of many processes will span multiple layers, and involve multiple parties. For example, the customer organization and the service integrator can both carry out elements of supplier management; the service integrator and service providers will each have responsibilities in the end to end change management process.

Each service provider might carry out individual process steps in a different way, but as part of an overall integrated process model. Process models are therefore important SIAM artefacts; local processes and work instructions are likely to remain within the domain of the individual organization who performs the activities.

Each party in a SIAM ecosystem should adapt and augment their own processes to integrate with the relevant process models, as part of the overall SIAM model.

The detail of the process models, and the allocation of activities to the different layers in the SIAM structure, will vary for each implementation of SIAM. See the SIAM Body of Knowledge, Section 2: SIAM Roadmap for more information on process models and how to design a SIAM model.

Because each SIAM model is different, this document cannot prescribe who will do what for each process. In all SIAM models, it is important to ensure that the roles and responsibilities, interface and dependencies of the customer, service integrator and service providers are mapped, clearly defined, and clearly understood.

B.2.1 Process Guides

The process guides in this document provide a generic description for each process, plus an illustration of the considerations that should be made when designing and using the process in a SIAM ecosystem.

Each process guide includes:
- Process purpose
- SIAM considerations
- Generic process information:
    - Activities
    - Example roles
    - Example metrics
    - Example inputs and outputs.

B.3 Common SIAM considerations

This section examines the considerations that are common for all processes in a SIAM ecosystem.

B.3.1 Complexity

In a SIAM ecosystem, processes can seem more complex due to factors including:

- Different layers have different accountabilities and responsibilities within the same process
- An increased number of parties is involved in end to end process execution
- The need to integrate different processes from multiple organizations to support the end to end process
- The number of interactions between processes from different organizations.

Complex processes are more difficult to understand and follow. Wherever possible, processes in a SIAM ecosystem should be designed to avoid complexity.

B.3.2 Who owns the End to End Process?

Defining process ownership and levels of accountability and responsibility will also be important in a SIAM ecosystem. Common factors here include:

- The customer is ultimately accountable for the outcomes of the processes, as they are the organization that commissions the SIAM ecosystem
- The service integrator is accountable for:
    - The overall design of the process models, supporting policies, and data and information standards. They must ensure that the design will deliver the required outcomes
    - Their own local processes and procedures
- The service providers are accountable for the design of their own local processes and procedures, ensuring that they comply with the process models, supporting policies, and data and information standards provided by the service integrator.

B.3.3 Toolset Considerations

The toolset(s) that will support processes need to be defined as part of the SIAM model. The decision about which toolset will be used and who will own it will be made during the Plan and Build stage of the SIAM roadmap.

Decisions need to be made about:

- Which toolset(s) will be used
- Who owns the toolset(s).

The outcome of these decisions will be documented in the tooling strategy. The decisions can only be made once the SIAM model has been finalized.

If the customer owns the toolset, it will make it less challenging to change the service integrator. Alternatively, using a toolset owned by an external service integrator might offer an opportunity to access a best of breed toolset.

B.3.4 Data and Information Considerations

B.3.4.1 Who Owns the Data?

This decision needs to take into consideration what happens if a service provider or a service integrator is replaced. The customer organization should aim to have ownership of, or guaranteed access to, any data that is necessary to operate the services; for example, incident records.

B.3.4.2 Who Owns the Intellectual Property on Artefacts?

As part of normal service operation in a SIAM ecosystem, artefacts will be created; for example, knowledge articles in the knowledge management repository.

Intellectual property rights for these artefacts need to be defined and agreed in contracts or service agreements. There will be commercial considerations to take into account, for example, a service provider may be unwilling to share their articles with another organization.

B.3.4.3 Is Data and Information Consistent?

The SIAM model should include standards for data and information, and supporting policies. A data dictionary will ensure all parties use common standards.

For example, there should be a minimum dataset for incidents and a standard definition of incident priorities and severities.

B.3.4.4 How is Access to Shared Data, Information, and Tools Controlled?

Policies and processes for access control need to be defined and managed, taking into account security considerations.

B.3.4.5 Who is Responsible for Process Improvement?

All parties in the SIAM ecosystem are responsible for improving their own processes, and for improving the end to end processes, facilitated by the service integrator.

The service integrator is responsible for ensuring that the processes from different service providers continue to work together within the overall process models.

The service integrator's process owners are accountable for end to end process improvement.

B.3.4 6 How will Compliance and Assurance be Managed?

Compliance and assurance requirements should be included in contracts so that they can be enforced.

The service integrator is accountable for assurance of process outcomes across the end to end processes.

B.4 Process Guide: Service Portfolio Management

B.4.1 Process Purpose

The purpose of service portfolio management is to maintain information on all services, to provide the customer organization with a better insight as to ongoing spend, and support business decisions on future investment in products and services.

The process creates a single source of service information, and tracks the status of planned, current and retired services.

B.4.2 SIAM Considerations

Service portfolio management considerations in a SIAM environment include:

- It is not possible to transition to a SIAM model without a clear definition of all services, service providers, dependencies and relationships between services, and service characteristics. Service portfolio management information is therefore critical to any SIAM implementation
- The customer organization should own the service portfolio. Responsibility for execution of the service portfolio management process can be given to the customer's retained capabilities, or delegated to the service integrator
- The portfolio needs to be kept current with information from all service providers, including potential new services arising from innovation opportunities. Service provider contracts need to include a requirement to provide this information
- Data and information standards for portfolio records need to be agreed and consistent across all service providers
- The service portfolio management process must be aligned with the processes for introducing and retiring new services and new service providers.

B.4.3 Generic Process Information

B.4.3.1 Activities

Service portfolio management activities can include:

- Creating a service portfolio
- Maintaining a service portfolio
- Reviewing a service portfolio.

B.4.3.2 Example Roles

Service portfolio management roles can include:

- Service portfolio manager.

B.4.3.3 Example Metrics

Service portfolio management metrics can include:

- Number of planned services
- Number of current services
- Number of retired services
- Commercial viability of services
- Number of portfolio opportunities.

B.4.3.4 Inputs and Outputs

Service portfolio management inputs can include:

- Customer strategy and requirements
- Demand management data
- Service portfolio reviews
- Service catalogues
- Service contracts
- New and changed services.

Service portfolio management outputs can include:

- Service portfolio
- Service portfolio reports
- Approved services
- Terminated services.

B.5 Process Guide: Monitoring and Measuring

B.5.1 Process Purpose

The purpose of the monitoring and measuring process includes:

- Responsibility for the monitoring and measurement of systems and service delivery
- Monitoring services against defined thresholds, creating alerts, identifying and predicting service impacting trends and preventing service interruptions
- Measuring service utilization and performance.

This process has relationships with other processes including event management and service level management.

B.5.2 SIAM Considerations

Monitoring and measuring considerations in a SIAM environment include:

- Assuring the ability of all service providers to monitor their services and underlying technical components
- The requirement for a data dictionary, data models, terminology, thresholds and reporting schedules that are consistent across the SIAM ecosystem
- Shared performance measures to enable end to end reporting.

B.5.3 Generic Process Information

B.5.3.1 Activities

Monitoring and measuring activities can include:

- Service monitoring
- Threshold detection
- Event creation
- Report creation
- Performance analysis
- Tuning.

B.5.3.2 Roles

Monitoring and measuring roles can include:

- Service level manager
- Capacity manager
- Availability manager
- Event manager
- Performance manager.

B.5.3.3 Example Metrics

Monitoring and measuring metrics can include:

- Incidents related to capacity/availability issues
- Availability of services
- Performance of services
- Reports issued within schedule.

B.5.3.4 Example Inputs and Outputs

Monitoring and measuring inputs can include:

- Contractual service levels
- Service thresholds
- Alerts
- Service provider data
- Reporting requirements, formats and frequencies.

Monitoring and measuring outputs can include:

- Measurement reports
- Service measurements
- Service improvement opportunities
- Events
- Forecasts
- Change requests.

B.6 Process Guide: Event Management

B.6.1 Process Purpose

Event management is the process by which events are identified through the monitoring of technology components, systems and services and, where appropriate, action is taken.

The process seeks to provide early detection and even avoidance of system and service outages, and increase service availability for users. It is closely related to monitoring and measuring, incident management, and availability management.

B.6.2 SIAM Considerations

Event management considerations in a SIAM environment include:

- The organizational design should include the function responsible for managing events. This could be a central function provided by the service integrator, a virtual function provided by all service providers, or individual functions in each service provider
- The rules for managing event thresholds should be defined in a policy that is consistent across all service providers; for example, at what point do repeated events concerning slow performance result in an incident being raised
- Specific tools may be required to collate events from multiple service providers, correlate the data, and apply rules to identify end to end issues
- Targets for event diagnosis and resolution should be common across service providers.

B.6.3 Generic Process Information

B.6.3.1 Activities

Event management activities can include:

- Record an event (often automatically created by monitoring systems)
- Diagnose and evaluate the event
- Create an associated incident if required, and assign to the incident management process
- Close the event
- Configure and tune event management tools.

B.6.3.2 Example Roles

Event management roles can include:

- Operations team
- Service desk.

B.6.3.3 Example Metrics

Event management metrics can include:

- Number of events, by type
- Accuracy of event information, by type
- Number of incidents avoided
- Number of failures resolved.

B.6.3.4 Example Inputs and Outputs

Event management inputs can include:

- Auto-generated alerts
- User reports of system failures.

Event management outputs can include:

- Event data
- Trend reports
- Input into related processes including incident and problem management.

B.7 Process Guide: Incident Management

B.7.1 Process Purpose

Incident management records and manages service issues (known as incidents) that are interrupting the availability of a service. The process also manages events that are degrading or could degrade service performance.

The process seeks to restore service. This is often within an agreed timescale, dictated by the priority of the incident, based on its impact and how quickly it needs to be resolved.

B.7.2 SIAM Considerations

Incident management considerations in a SIAM environment include:

- The incident management process model needs to support prompt restoration of service. This includes routing incidents to potential resolvers as quickly as possible, and with the minimum number of parties involved. The associated service desk model needs to support this
- Data and information standards for incident records, incident transfer, and supporting tooling must be defined, to support the effective referral of incidents between service providers
- Incident priorities and severities should be defined consistently across all parties
- Roles and responsibilities must be defined for coordinating incident investigations that involve multiple service providers
- Targets for incident resolution need to recognize that incidents may be referred between service providers. The referrals will take time, and each service provider will have their own agreed targets. The end to end process needs to make sure that customer targets are not breached, even if every provider achieves their own target
- There is a risk that service providers may refer incidents to another service provider to avoid breaching a resolution time service level
- Incident management teams from different providers are likely to be in different geographical locations, creating challenges for collaboration on incidents.

B.7.3 Generic Process Information

B.7.3.1 Activities

Incident management activities can include:
- Incident reporting
- Incident detection
- Incident categorisation and prioritization
- Record creation
- Incident investigation
- Incident resolution
- Confirmation of resolution
- Record updated and closed
- Incident trend analysis.

B.7.3.2 Example Roles

Incident management roles can include:
- Incident manager
- Service desk
- Major incident manager
- Technical staff.

B.7.3.3 Example Metrics

Incident management metrics can include:
- Number of incidents (overall, by service, by site etc.)
- Number of incidents resolved at first point of contact
- Incidents that needed to be reopened
- Customer satisfaction with the incident management process
- Incidents that have been incorrectly assigned.

B.7.3.4 Example Inputs and Outputs

Incident management inputs can include:
- Events
- User reports.

Incident management outputs can include:
- Incident records
- Resolved incidents
- Incident reports
- Incident metrics.

B.8 Process Guide: Problem Management

B.8.1 Process Purpose

Problem management is responsible for managing the lifecycle of a problem, which is defined as the unknown underlying cause of an incident.

It is also responsible for preventing incidents and problems from occurring or recurring.

The problem management process has both reactive and proactive aspects: the reactive aspect is concerned with solving problems in response to one or more incidents within an agreed timescale and based on the priority of the problem. The proactive aspect is concerned with preventing incidents from occurring in the first place.

B.8.2 SIAM Considerations

Problem management considerations in a SIAM environment include:

- Getting all parties to take part in problem management working groups and forums, including joint working to resolve problems that involve multiple service providers
- Coordinating problem investigation and resolution activities across multiple service providers
- Encouraging and facilitating the sharing of data and information on problems with other service providers
- Aligning targets for problem resolution across service providers
- Creating and using common terminology, data and information standards, and problem classifications across service providers.

B.8.3 Generic Process Information

B.8.3.1 Activities

Problem management activities can include:

- Review of incident(s) reported or trend analysis of incident records
- Creating problem records
- Categorising and prioritizing problem records
- Identifying and communicating workarounds
- Identifying and addressing the root cause of a problem
- Proactively identifying and addressing potential problems.

B.8.3.2 Sample Roles

Problem management roles can include:

- Problem manager
- Technical teams.

B.8.3.3 Example Metrics

Problem management metrics can include:

- Problems recorded per month – proactive and reactive
- Number of in-progress problems
- Number of resolved problems
- Number of recurring incidents while a problem is being investigated.

B.8.3.4 Example Inputs and Outputs

Problem management inputs can include:

- Incident records
- Configuration management information
- Change records
- Workarounds.

Problem management outputs can include:

- Problem records
- Problem reviews
- Resolved problems
- Workarounds
- Change requests
- Service improvements
- Knowledge articles
- Reports.

B.9 Process Guide: Change and Release Management

B.9.1 Process Purpose

Change management enables changes to be made to services with minimal amounts of disruption.

A release is a collection of one or more changes tested and deployed together. Release management ensures that the integrity of the live environment is protected and that the correct changes are deployed.

Together, the processes ensure that consistent methods are used to assess, approve and deploy changes.

B.9.2 SIAM Considerations

Change and release management considerations in a SIAM environment include:

Change management:

- The scope of change management needs to be clearly defined. The process can encompass many areas, including:
    - Technology
    - Processes
    - Policies
    - Organizational structures
    - The SIAM model
- Common standards should be developed for data and information and included in a change policy. For example, types of change, approval levels and notice periods
- The roles and parties involved in reviewing and approving changes must be clearly defined, and should include all organizations who may be affected by the change
- Consideration should be given to:
    - Having different reviewers and approvers for different types and classes of change. Who approves a change should depend on risk and impact, and if the change is an emergency
    - Allowing service providers to approve their own proven low risk, repeatable changes that don't affect other service providers
    - Leveraging automated testing and deployment techniques to reduce the level of manual review required and improve change success rates

Release management

- Release planning and implementation needs to consider all the affected service providers, and the customer organization. This includes coordinating and scheduling releases to avoid negative impact
- Responsibilities for testing integration between services from different service providers should be defined
- There should be a consistent format and method for communicating information about releases.

B.9.3 Generic Process Information

B.9.3.1 Activities

Change and release management activities can include:

- Analysis of proposed changes
- Approving changes
- Scheduling of changes
- Communication
- Packaging of releases
- Scheduling of releases
- Testing of releases
- Implementation and deployment
- Reviewing successful deployment.

B.9.3.2 Example Roles

Change and release management roles can include:

- Change requestor
- Change manager
- Release manager
- Test manager
- Product owners
- Change advisory board attendees.

B.9.3.3 Example Metrics

Change and release management metrics can include:

- Changes per month
- Successful changes/releases
- Emergency changes
- Failed changes/releases
- Number of incidents caused by changes.

B.9.3.4 Sample Inputs and Outputs

Change and release management inputs can include:

- Change policy
- Release policy
- Requests for change
- Incident and problem data related to changes
- Service targets
- Test results
- Configuration information
- Change and release plans.

Change and release management outputs can include:

- Approved/rejected changes
- Change schedules
- Change/release communications
- Release plans
- Service availability plans
- Change reviews.

B.10 Process Guide: Configuration Management

B.10.1 Process Purpose

The purpose of configuration management is to identify, record, maintain and assure data and information about configuration items (CIs).

A configuration item can be anything used to deliver or support the services, including:

- A service
- Software application or product
- Hardware component
- Documentation.

The types of CIs in scope are tailored on a customer by customer basis. There can be many different types of CI.

CI details are often held in one or more configuration management databases (CMDB). Aggregation of multiple CMDBs and other data sources is referred to as a configuration management system (CMS).

Configuration management records and maintains details of the relationships between CIs, and documents how they interact and rely upon each other.

Configuration management has interfaces with other processes, including:

- Incident management, which registers incidents against CIs, and uses CI information to identify existing incidents for the affected CI or recent changes to it that may have cause an incident
- Change management, which registers changes against CIs and uses configuration management data to assess the potential impact of changes
- Problem management, which uses configuration management information to look for incident trends.

B.10.2 SIAM Considerations

Configuration management considerations in a SIAM environment include:

- The scope of the service integrator's CMDB must be clear, and should only contain data that the service integrator needs to fulfil its responsibilities

- Service provider contracts and agreements need to stipulate what configuration management data they are required to provide
- Each organization is responsible for maintaining its own CMDB, containing the data necessary to support delivery of its own services
- Service providers need to share a subset of the data in their CMDB with the service integrator and other service providers, to support delivery of the end to end service
- A policy should be defined to specify common classifications and record contents for any configuration data that needs to be shared across parties in the SIAM ecosystem
- The approach, toolset integration, and access control for sharing CMDB data between different parties needs careful consideration
- Where CMDB data is shared, responsibility for maintaining shared items must be defined
- Responsibilities for assessing and improving data quality and CMDB accuracy should be defined.

B.10.3 Generic Process Information

B.10.3.1 Activities

Configuration management activities can include:

- Design and implementation of configuration management database(s)
- Gathering data to populate CMDB(s)
- Updating data based on triggers including change management inputs
- Audit of configuration management data
- Documentation and investigation of any data discrepancies
- Providing reports as required.

B.10.3.2 Example Roles

Configuration management roles can include:

- Configuration manager
- Configuration analyst.

B.10.3.3 Example Metrics

Configuration management metrics can include:

- Number of configuration items (CIs), by service provider, type, status etc.
- Number of CI to CI relationships (by service)
- Number of CIs with incomplete or missing information
- CIs that are verified/unverified
- CIs discovered that are not in the CMDB
- CIs in the CMDB that should be seen by automated discovery tools but are not.

B.10.3.4 Example inputs and outputs

Configuration management inputs can include:

- Data from discovery tools
- Data and information from physical checks
- Incident records
- Change records
- Build information from infrastructure teams
- Application information from development teams.

Configuration management outputs can include:

- CMDB records
- Verification schedules
- Verification reports.

B.11 Process Guide: Service Level Management

B.11.1 Process Purpose

Service level management (SLM) ensures that service performance meets agreed requirements. These requirements are set out as service level targets in a contract or service agreement.

SLM contributes to, reviews and validates the service level targets against service provider capability and planned service provision.

Following the implementation of services, SLM will continually review, report on, and drive performance against the targets.

B.11.2 SIAM Considerations

Service level management considerations in a SIAM environment include:

- Service providers need to recognize that the service integrator is acting as the agent of the customer and work with them on SLM activities and reporting
- The scope of SLM should be clearly defined. Its activities need to be distinct from those of:
    - Supplier management
    - Contract management
    - Performance management
    - Business relationship management,
  even if performed in the same layer. The interfaces between these processes should be mapped
- SLM needs to include thresholds to define when a breach of performance should be escalated to supplier management, so the process can apply remedies
- The SIAM model needs to reflect any service level targets that may have been agreed before the service integrator was appointed
- The scope of the contracted services, and any dependencies on services from other service providers, must be clearly defined
- An approach must be established to manage the situation where the failure of a service provider to meet their targets is due to another service provider
- The service integrator will need information to verify the service providers' performance reports. This may need to be sourced from other service providers and from service consumers

- It can be challenging to produce consolidated reports unless the service level targets of all service providers are aligned. For example: a common definition and calculation of 'availability', and reports covering the same time periods
- Consideration should be given to including internal service providers within the scope of SLM.

B.11.3 Generic process information

B.11.3.1 Activities

Service level management activities can include:

- Tracking performance against service level targets
- Validating service reports from service providers
- Producing and publishing reports of service achievements against service levels and of trends
- Reviewing performance data to identify improvement opportunities
- Reviewing service level targets for ongoing alignment with business requirements.

B.11.3.2 Example Roles

Service level management roles can include:

- Service level manager
- Reporting analyst.

B.11.3.3 Example Metrics

Service level management metrics can include:

- Customer perception of the services
- Service level achievement against targets.

Service level management metrics are often trended on a monthly, quarterly, and annual basis. This can highlight areas for improvement and successes.

B.11.3.4 Example Inputs and Outputs

Service level management inputs can include:

- Contracts
- Service targets
- Service provider capabilities
- Service performance data
- Customer feedback.

Service level management outputs can include:

- Service level reports
- Trend analysis
- Service improvement opportunities.

B.12 Process Guide: Supplier Management

B.12.1 Process Purpose

The supplier management process defines the supplier management policy and strategy, establishes a management framework, and identifies and manages service providers, to deliver value for money to the customer.

The process manages supplier performance, in conjunction with service level management and contract management.

B.12.2 SIAM Considerations

The 'suppliers' in a SIAM ecosystem are referred to as service providers.

Supplier management considerations in a SIAM environment include:

- Effective supplier management is critical to the success of any SIAM implementation. Performance issues with one service provider can affect others, as well as the end to end service
- Supplier management is normally executed by the service integrator, acting on behalf of the customer
- Supplier management should be clearly defined as separate from contract management and service level management, even if performed in the same layer. The interfaces between these processes should be clear
- This process should manage service provider performance escalations received from the service level management process
- A supplier management policy should be created that is appropriate for and fair to different types and sizes of service providers
- The execution of the process should not favour one service provider over others. This can be a challenge if the service integrator is also a service provider, or where some service providers are internal
- There should be a clear definition for when the supplier management process can apply remedies, and when a breach of performance becomes a breach of contract that should be escalated to contract management
- A mechanism should be developed to apportion remedies for failure to meet service level targets where multiple service providers contributed to the failure
- Non-financial incentives can be as effective as financial remedies to drive appropriate service provider behaviour
- Supplier forums can assist in creating a collaborative culture.

B.12.3 Generic Process Information

B.12.3.1 Activities

Supplier management activities can include:
- Plan, produce and implement a supplier management policy and process
- Enforce the policy
- Design and implement a supplier management framework
- Apply remedies for failure to meet service level targets
- Identify and manage non-conformity to the policy and process
- Escalate to contract management as required.

B.12.3.2 Example Roles

Supplier management roles can include:
- Supplier manager
- Account manager
- Procurement manager
- Service provider service manager.

B.12.3.3 Example Metrics

Supplier management metrics can include:
- Number of suppliers managed in accordance with the policy
- Supplier performance aligned to committed performance targets
- Reduction of service failures
- Accuracy of service reporting and conformity to service level agreements.

B.12.3.4 Example Inputs and Outputs

Supplier management inputs can include:
- Business policy requirements
- Contracts
- Audit reports
- Regulatory and industry standards
- Previous breaches and achievements
- Customer and supplier requirements
- Planned changes
- Project plans and risk logs

Supplier management outputs can include:

- Supplier conformance reports
- Planned improvements and remediation activities
- Training needs.

B.13 Process Guide: Contract Management

B.13.1 Process Purpose

The purpose of contract management is to:

- Evaluate proposals from prospective service providers
- Negotiate and finalise contracts with service providers
- Verify if contractual requirements are being met, and trigger contractual remediation if required
- Assess if contracts are still relevant, and advise on updates or termination if no longer required.

B.13.2 SIAM Considerations

Contract management considerations in a SIAM environment include:

- The customer is always accountable for contract management; they hold the contracts with the service providers. Some organizations delegate responsibility for execution of some activities to an external service integrator, or use them as an advisor
- Contract management should be clearly defined as separate from supplier management and service level management, even if performed in the same layer. The interfaces between these processes should be clear
- A SIAM ecosystem requires appropriate contracts to avoid vendor lock in, provide for shared goals, shared risk and reward, end to end service levels and performance measures, collaboration, and the right of the service integrator to act on behalf of the customer
- Clearly define when a breach of performance becomes a breach of contract. This process is responsible for managing breaches of contract
- Ensure that contract breaches are addressed consistently and fairly with all service providers
- Implement practices to support management of multiple contracts, including a contract repository with associated access management.

B.13.3 Generic Process Information

B.13.3.1 Activities

Contract management activities can include:

- Negotiate and agree contracts
- Develop and implement sourcing strategies
- Manage contractual changes
- Verify delivery against contractual requirements
- Address contractual non-compliance.

B.13.3.2 Example Roles

Contract management roles can include:

- Contract manager
- Legal advisor.

B.13.3.3 Example Metrics

Contract management metrics can include:

- Contract renewals within schedule
- Service provider performance against contracts
- Contract breaches.

B.13.3.4 Example Inputs and Outputs

Contract management inputs can include:

- New service portfolio entries
- Contract framework
- Contract change notices
- Escalations from supplier management.

Contract management outputs can include:

- Service provider addition and removal plans
- Service improvement plans for under-performing service providers
- Contracts
- Warning notices
- Sourcing strategies.

B.14 Process Guide: Business Relationship Management

B.14.1 Process Purpose

The business relationship management (BRM) process is responsible for building and maintaining strong relationships between service providers and the consumers of their services.

BRM's role is to understand how business processes are supported by a service provider's services and processes. BRM is also responsible for ensuring the right messages are received by the right stakeholders at the right time.

BRM's goal is to create convergence between IT services and business needs, acting as a strategic advisor, not a supporting function.

B.14.2 SIAM Considerations

BRM considerations in a SIAM environment include:

- The retained capabilities within the customer organization are normally responsible for BRM with the service consumers
- The service integrator may have its own BRM function that has a relationship with the customer organization's retained capabilities, but this is normally part of the service integrator's commercial activities and doesn't necessarily form part of the SIAM model
- Service providers may also have BRM functions, which may also be outside the scope of the SIAM model
- A BRM policy should be developed to ensure consistent communication and stakeholder management
- The business areas that consume services must understand that their point of contact for services is via the customer's retained capabilities, and not directly with the service providers.

B.14.3 Generic Process Information

B.14.3.1 Activities

BRM activities can include:

- Developing and maintaining stakeholder engagement plans
- Developing and maintaining communication plans
- Meeting with the service integrator, service providers and customers
- Establishing and maintaining stakeholder forums
- Executing communication plans
- Reviewing customer satisfaction.

B.14.3.2 Example Roles

BRM roles can include:

- Business relationship managers
- Communication managers
- Service owners
- Service managers
- Stakeholders.

B.14.3.3 Example Metrics

BRM metrics can include:

- Delivery of communication management plan
- Delivery of communication improvement plans
- Number of improvement initiatives
- Number of satisfaction surveys
- Ratings from satisfaction surveys.

B.14.3.4 Example Inputs and Outputs

BRM inputs can include:

- Communication standards, including templates, logos, and style sheets
- Stakeholder map
- Communication plan
- Customer feedback.

BRM outputs can include:

- Communication plan
- Business communications
- Minutes of meetings
- Customer satisfaction reports
- Improvement plans.

B.15 Process Guide: Financial Management

B.15.1 Process Purpose

The purpose of financial management is to oversee the management of the end to end financial function and the activities of collating, investigating, analysing and presenting financial information to the customer.

B.15.2 SIAM Considerations

Financial management considerations in a SIAM environment include:

- Maintaining commercial confidentiality across the ecosystem
- Being able to compare and contrast financial information from different services providers in a meaningful way
- Understanding the cost of a service provided by multiple service providers, including the cost drivers of different components
- Presenting consolidated financial information to the customer in an understandable format
- Maintaining traceability of financial information across the SIAM ecosystem.

B.15.3 Generic Process Information

B.15.3.1 Activities

There are 6 main financial management activities:

- Costing
- Budget planning
- Monthly monitoring of spend against budget
- Produce and maintain financial reports and outputs
- Conduct financial impact analysis
- Process invoices.

B.15.3.2 Example Roles

Financial management roles can include:

- Chief financial officer
- Management accountant
- Cost accountant
- Accounts assistant.

B.15.3.3 Example Metrics

Financial management metrics can include:

- Cost of a service
- Profitability of a service
- Comparison between services and service providers
- Spend against budget
- Accuracy of invoices
- Resolution of invoice discrepancies
- Outputs produced on time.

B.15.3.4 Example Inputs and Outputs

Financial management inputs can include:

- Invoices
- Budget plans
- Contractual pricing models
- Purchase orders
- Service costs.

Financial management outputs can include:

- Billing plan
- Reports
- Cost breakdown
- Spend and forecast data
- Financial risk and opportunity information
- Invoices.

B.16 Process Guide: Information Security Management

B.16.1 Process Purpose

Information security management (ISM) sets and monitors adherence to security policies and processes. It manages the confidentiality, integrity, and availability of information, data, IT and people.

Its objective is to protect individuals, technology, and organizations from damage caused by system outages, breaches of privacy, malicious attacks, and loss or disclosure of protected data and information.

B.16.2 SIAM Considerations

Information security management considerations in a SIAM environment include:

- Defining who is accountable for establishing and managing the end to end information security process and policies
- Using consistent information security classifications and definitions. For example, what constitutes a security incident?
- Managing and communicating breaches and identified vulnerabilities across the ecosystem
- Defining responsibility for managing the investigation and resolution of security breaches involving multiple parties
- Including security targets within service provider contracts, for example, giving the authority to suspend a service provider's service if it is compromising other services
- Being aware of increased security risks when lower level risks are aggregated across multiple parties.

B.16.3 Generic Process Information

B.16.3.1 Activities

Information security management activities can include:

- Plan, produce and implement an ISM policy and process
- Enforce the policy and monitor adherence
- Implement a security toolset
- Monitor security activity and take appropriate resolution or improvement actions
- Identify risks derived from aggregation of lower level risks

- Raise incidents for breaches and failures using the incident management process and service desk
- Evaluate and update the policy, process and tools to ensure protection is maintained
- Plan and deliver training, audits, reviews and tests of the security framework.

B.16.3.2 Example Roles

Information security management roles can include:

- Senior information risk officer
- Information security manager
- Service desk
- Incident manager.

B.16.3.3 Example Metrics

Information security management metrics can include:

- Number of security-related incidents
- Number of security breaches
- Percentage of users complying with security training and other requirements
- Availability and accuracy of security tools and systems
- Accuracy and outcomes of security audits and tests
- Percentage awareness of security principles throughout the organization.

B.16.3.4 Example Inputs and Outputs

Information security management inputs can include:

- Policy requirements
- Regulatory and industry standards
- Previous breach and 'near miss' information
- Planned changes
- Customer and service provider requirements
- Project plans
- Risk logs.

Information security management outputs can include:

- Security incident records
- Planned improvements
- Remediation activities
- Training needs
- Disciplinary and human resources action
- Process and policy status reports.

B.17 Process Guide: Continual Service Improvement

B.17.1 Process Purpose

The purpose of continual service improvement is to provide a consistent method of quantifying, tracking and managing the delivery of improvement activity across an ecosystem.

Improvement activities can be applied to people, processes, services, technology, and the interfaces and relationships between them.

B.17.2 SIAM Considerations

Continual service improvement considerations in a SIAM environment include:

- There should be a common definition of continual service improvement across all parties in the ecosystem
- Continual service improvement should be on the agenda of governance boards
- Continual service improvement should be the primary focus of the process forum structural elements
- All service providers should be encouraged and incentivised to contribute to continual service improvement activities
- There should be an approach to share lessons learned across all parties in the SIAM ecosystem
- There may be a need to a central database or register of continual service improvement activities
- The service integrator will be responsible for managing cross-service provider improvements
- There needs to be a mechanism in place to prioritize improvements to the end to end services and processes.

B.17.3 Generic Process Information

B.17.3.1 Activities

Continual service improvement activities can include:

- Investigation: the improvement is identified and further information obtained
- Baseline: document current metrics
- Identify and quantify the expected or desired improvements and benefits

- Categorize and prioritize the improvement, to define the required level of governance and relative importance
- Approve further activity
- Stakeholder management and communication planning
- Plan improvement
- Carry out improvement actions
- Review improvement
- Measure, review, and quantify benefit
- Close improvement action, including documenting lessons learned.

B.17.3.2 Example Roles

Continual service improvement roles can include:

- Improvement initiator
- Improvement sponsor
- Improvement implementer
- Governance board attendees
- Process forum attendees.

B.17.3.3 Example Metrics

Continual service improvement metrics can include:

- Number of improvements identified, active, and completed
- Cost of improvement activities
- Increased value associated with improvement activities
- Improvements in achievement of service level targets and process performance indicators.

B.17.3.4 Example Inputs and Outputs

Continual service improvement inputs can include:

- Management information including service level reports, internal key performance indicator reporting, trend analysis
- Lessons learned reviews
- Audits
- Customer satisfaction reports
- Strategic drivers including delivery model evaluation, industry bench marking, governance board outputs
- Improvement register
- Management information and recommendations
- Status changes to logged improvements.

B.18 Process Guide: Knowledge Management

B.18.1 Process Purpose

Knowledge Management is the process of capturing knowledge and making it available in a controlled and quality-assured manner to all appropriate people.

B.18.2 SIAM Considerations

Knowledge management considerations in a SIAM environment include:

- Standardised templates and definitions for knowledge can be useful to ensure consistent capture and dissemination
- Service providers should be encouraged to share knowledge with each other
- Responsibilities for creating, reviewing, approving, publishing, and maintaining knowledge articles must be clearly defined
- Relevant parties must be able to access knowledge, either from a single knowledge repository, or a virtual repository linking all providers
- Knowledge should be consistent across the SIAM ecosystem.

B.18.3 Generic Process Information

B.18.3.1 Activities

Knowledge management activities can include:

- Knowledge identification, capture and maintenance
- Knowledge transfer
- Data and information management
- Evaluation and improvement.

B.18.3.2 Example Roles

Knowledge management roles can include:

- Knowledge creator
- Knowledge manager
- Knowledge editor.

B.18.3.3 Example Metrics

Knowledge management metrics can include:

- Number of knowledge users
- Reduction in incident resolution time owing to use of knowledge items
- Percentage of incidents resolved by referral to knowledge items
- Number of active knowledge articles
- Frequency of updates
- Frequency of access by article
- Accuracy of repository content
- Reduction in time spent on knowledge rediscovery.

B.18.3.4 Example Inputs and Outputs

Knowledge management inputs can include:

- Documented observations
- External knowledge sources
- Data and process information
- Data repositories
- Release notes
- Procedures manuals
- Training material.

Knowledge management outputs can include:

- Knowledge articles
- Reports
- Updated knowledge management system
- Archived data and information
- Updated training materials.

B.19 Process Guide: Toolset and Information Management

B.19.1 Process Purpose

The purpose of toolset and information management is to provide toolset(s) to support the other processes, facilitate information sharing, and manage data, information, and knowledge.

B.19.2 SIAM Considerations

In SIAM models, there may be a single toolset, or many toolsets. Toolset and information management considerations in a SIAM environment include:

- Defining and managing the use of consistent standards for data, information, and knowledge across all service providers
- Creating the toolset strategy for the SIAM model
- Creating an enterprise toolset architecture for the SIAM ecosystem
- Selecting an appropriate toolset in line with the strategy and enterprise architecture
- Defining, implementing, and maintaining integration between the toolsets of different parties.

B.19.3 Generic Process Information

B.19.3.1 Activities

Toolset and information management activities can include:
- Toolset selection
- Toolset implementation
- Toolset management and maintenance
- Data and information standards definition
- Toolset integration.

B.19.3.2 Example Roles

Toolset and information management roles can include:
- Toolset architect
- Toolset developer
- Toolset manager
- Data and information architect
- Data and information manager
- Toolset service provider.

B.19.3.3 Example Metrics

Toolset and information management metrics can include:

- Toolset availability
- Toolset reliability
- Toolset data quality.

B.19.3.4 Example Inputs and Outputs

Toolset and information management inputs can include:

- Configuration data
- Interface schema and designs
- User data
- Data repositories.

Toolset and information management outputs can include:

- Toolset
- Performance reports
- Service level reports
- Data and information standards
- Data dictionary
- Data interchange standards
- Information classification.

B.20 Process Guide: Project Management

B.20.1 Process Purpose

The purpose of project management is to provide a structured approach that delivers projects on time, on budget and at the appropriate level of quality.

B.20.2 SIAM Considerations

Project management in a SIAM environment manages the end to end outcomes of projects across multiple service providers.

Considerations include:

- The increased complexity of project relationships within a SIAM ecosystem
- Accounting for the fact that there is no direct contractual relationships the service integrator and service providers
- Planning integrated projects involving multiple project teams in multiple service providers
- Obtaining consistency in reporting project status and progress
- Establishment of a collaborative culture to support cross-service provider project management
- Managing risks in integrated projects
- Ensuring effective acceptance into service criteria for project implementations across multiple service providers.

B.20.3 Generic Process Information

B.20.3.1 Activities

Project management activities can include:

- Planning
- Adhering to organizational policies and requirements
- Directing actions
- Status reporting
- Risk and issue management
- Delivery of change requests
- Quality management of deliverables
- Managing stakeholders.

B.20.3.2 Example Roles

Project management roles can include:

- Project director
- Project manager
- Project management office.

B.20.3.3 Example Metrics

Project management metrics can include:

- Delivery against plan
- Delivery against quality requirements
- Delivery against budget
- Overdue products
- Customer satisfaction.

B.20.3.4 Example Inputs and Outputs

Project management inputs can include:

- Proposals
- Purchase orders
- Project plans
- Project change requests
- Customer requirements
- Quality criteria.

Project management outputs can include:

- Completed projects
- Delivered products
- Plans
- Tasks
- Lessons learned.

B.21 Process Guide: Audit and Control

B.21.1 Process Purpose

The purpose of audit and control is to provide assurance that the services provided to the customer are being delivered in accordance with documented requirements. This can include contracted, legislative, regulatory, and security requirements.

B.21.2 SIAM Considerations

Audit and control considerations in a SIAM environment include:

- It is desirable to apply the same governance framework across all parties, however this may not be possible for certain service providers, for example commodity cloud service providers
- Each organization should own its risks, however the overall accountability for who will ensure that these have been addressed needs to be clearly defined
- The roles of the customer and service integrator in ensuring security assurance and compliance need to be clearly defined
- Requirements need to be in a format that can be understood by auditors, and must be clear enough to verify if they are being met
- Audits will need to take place across the whole SIAM ecosystem
- Audits should be conducted on integrated processes involving several service providers, as well as on individual service provider processes
- The rights of the service integrator (or another organization) to carry out audits should be included in contracts with service providers.

B.21.3 Generic Process Information

B.21.3.1 Activities

Audit and control activities can include:

- Auditing an organization's processes and systems
- Quality assurance planning
- Auditing projects
- Identifying non-conformance against requirements
- Recording, presenting, and managing audit findings
- Tracking non-conformances through to closure.

B.21.3.2 Example Roles

Audit and control roles can include:

- Quality manager
- Chief security officer
- Auditor
- Process owner.

B.21.3.3 Example Metrics

Audit and control metrics can include:

- Compliance against requirements
- Number of non-conformances identified, opened, and closed.

B.21.3.4 Example Inputs and Outputs

Audit and control inputs can include:

- Audit scope
- Requirements
- Policies
- Standards
- Processes
- Data and information records
- Performance reports
- Process metrics.

Audit and control outputs consist of audit reports, including:

- Audit scope
- Non-conformances
- Evidence
- Observations
- Risks and issues
- Improvement opportunities.